THE UNAUTHORIZED GUIDE TO DOING BUSINESS THE

SIMON COWELL

WAY

10 SECRETS OF THE INTERNATIONAL MUSIC MOGUL

By Trevor Clawson

D0910722

CAPSTONE

This edition first published 2011
© 2011 Trevor Clawson

The Unauthorized Guide to Doing Business the Simon Cowell Way is an unofficial, independent publication, and Capstone Publishing Ltd is not endorsed, sponsored, affiliated with or otherwise authorized by Simon Cowell.

Registered office
Capstone Publishing Ltd. (A Wiley Company), The Atrium, Southern Gate, Chichester, West Sussex, PO19 8SQ, United Kingdom

For details of our global editorial offices, for customer services and for information about how to apply for permission to reuse the copyright material in this book please see our website at www.wiley.com.

Library of Congress Cataloguing-in-Publication Data

9780857081285

A catalogue record for this book is available from the British Library.

Set in Myriad Pro by Sparks (www.sparkspublishing.com)
Printed in Great Britain by TJ International Ltd, Padstow, Cornwall

CONTENTS

Simon Cowell's status as one of the most powerful men in the record industry has been achieved on the back of a recent run of TV shows, but he spent many years learning the music business from the bottom up.

Successful marketing depends on a close and intimate knowledge of your target consumers and what they want. Over the years, Cowell has honed his market research methods.

THE LIFE AND TIMES OF SIMON COWELL

Simon Cowell wears a lot of hats. To the millions of viewers who watch his performances on US and UK television, he is first and foremost a media personality, trading on his wits and charisma as he passes judgement on the thousands of talent show hopefuls who cross his path every year. To those with an interest in the music industry he is an innovative talent scout who has perfected the art of discovering, moulding and marketing new singers and bands under the glare of the TV cameras. And for ratings-hungry network managers, he is a producer with the golden touch. At a time when broadcasters are fighting to maintain audience share against a backdrop of proliferating specialist channels, Cowell is the man who can deliver stellar viewing figures on the Saturday nights when his shows are aired.

Cowell is all these things and something more. Since he first appeared on television on the UK talent show *Pop Idol*, Cowell's reputation as a formidable businessman has been on a rising curve. Open a tabloid newspaper or entertainment industry trade publication and the chances are you'll come across a picture of a smiling Cowell, but you'll also find no shortage of stories about his activities in the rarified pages of the *Financial Times* and *Wall Street Journal*. He is no longer a humble television producer cum music business executive. He is a major player in a multi billion pound industry and his business methods have won huge respect.

He is also a very rich man. In November 2009, US business magazine *Forbes* named Simon Cowell television's best paid man, beating real estate billionaire Donald Trump into second place.

Forbes estimated that in the year between June 2008 and June 2009, Cowell earned around £45m, a figure comprised of cash from TV appearances in the UK and the US. The figure included his income from *American Idol* – the most popular series on US prime-time TV with an average weekly audience of 27 million – as well as the money he made from his music production, publishing work, fees for the production of his TV shows, plus, of course, record releases.

In the US, Cowell was paid more than £6m in 2009 for his work on *X Factor* while in the US Fox shelled out £20m for his services on *American Idol*. Off-screen, his work for Sony (Cowell's label Syco Music is part of Sony's global empire) made him £10m. At a time when the music industry is wrestling with falling revenues, Sony owes a lot to Cowell. According to *The Times* newspaper[1], Syco is responsible for record sales totalling 150 million units.

The breakdown of those figures – income from TV appearances and production coupled with money earned from record sales and music publishing – points to the underlying secret of Cowell's success. His broadcast and music careers don't run in parallel – they are inextricably bound together. The success of one is fed by the success of the other.

THE DOUBLE

Fast forward from November's article in *Forbes* to December of the same year. Christmas is coming and the latest UK series of the all-conquering pop talent show *X Factor* has reached its climax, with viewers choosing a winner in the youthful and indisputably likeable figure of the Newcastle teenager Joe McElderry. Flushed with success, the young man returns to the stage to sing the song that is to be released as his first single. With Christmas just a couple of weeks away, the record will be in the shops and available for download within a matter of days. If history is any guide, the momentum generated by Britain's most popular Saturday night TV show will carry it straight to the top of the charts. McElderry may or may not go on to have a long-term career in the music industry but for today at least he is king of the pop music castle.

Meanwhile, the power behind the throne is smiling happily. And as creator, producer and star of *X Factor*, Simon Cowell has good reason to look pleased. Not only is he paid handsomely by Independent Television (ITV) for a show that dominates Saturday night viewing figures, in the run up to Christmas his record company will release the fresh-faced winner's debut single and any subsequent recordings.

Let's just think about that for a moment. As a TV producer Cowell is paid to provide the ITV network with a popular programme that begins with thousands of hopeful contestants queuing up to audition in front of a judging panel. In the weeks and months that follow, the numbers will be whittled down until just twelve remain, entering a phase, in which one contestant is voted out every week. When the winner is finally announced he or she is already a nationally known figure and hit records are pretty much guaranteed. In other words, Cowell is paid by the TV company to discover individuals who have the potential to be future stars. Once the process is complete, the records made by the winners will further boost his bank balance. It's a double and very loud ringing of the cash register.

It's a business model that extends well beyond *X Factor*. Although he has now left the show to focus on a US *X Factor*, he is known to millions as the acerbic judge on *American Idol*. Here too he had the right to sign the winning artists to his label.

Meanwhile, in a variation on the *X Factor* theme, Cowell is also reaping the benefits of a more generalist TV talent show format.

Looking beyond singers to a realm of light entertainment that also includes dancers, comedians, jugglers and performing dogs, the '*Got Talent*' format has been successful in the UK, the US and around the world.

The *Got Talent* proposition – similar in respects to that of *X Factor* – leads the viewer on a journey running from open auditions, through a knockout phase to a grand finale in which a winner is chosen. In contrast to *X Factor*, the prize is not necessarily a record deal. But if the winner – or any other popular contestant – happens to be a singer, then Cowell once again has first option on a record deal.

Witness the worldwide phenomenon that is Susan Boyle. Appearing on the British version of the show – *Britain's Got Talent* – she was a genuine surprise. A middle aged woman from Scotland, she was initially greeted with scepticism from the judges. That scepticism vanished when she opened her mouth to deliver a powerful performance of 'I Dreamed a Dream'. Within days she was an internet sensation and although she didn't win the contest, she was signed up by Cowell and released a top selling debut album in 2009.

A MULTI MEDIA PLAYER

Cowell's business model – which sees him standing colossus fashion with one foot on the television industry and the other on the music business – has not only made him wealthy, it has made him an influential and powerful figure in the wider entertainment industry.

A good percentage of that power stems directly from the popularity of the shows that he creates and often – but not always – appears in. *X Factor* for example attracts audiences of 13 and 14 million on Saturday nights. Those figures would have been high in the 1960s and 1970s when viewers in the UK had a choice of just two or three channels; but in an age of multi-channel broadcasting and fragmented audiences, the fact that a single show can attract so many people is little short of miraculous.

In other words, Cowell is paid by the TV company to discover individuals who have the potential to be future stars. Once the process is complete, the records made by the winners will further boost his bank balance. It's a double pay-out.

It's a miracle that has been something of a lifesaver for ITV. All of the old networks have lost audience share to a plethora of new digital channels, a trend that was putting pressure on advertising revenues even before the 2008/2009 recession. But with *X Factor* covering the vital winter months and *Britain's Got Talent* pulling in viewers earlier in the year, ITV chiefs have been enjoying audience figures they can really shout about. That in turn has pushed up ad revenues. According to *The Times*, a thirty second slot during the *X Factor* finals cost £250,000 in 2009[2].

But the real source of Cowell's power as a media player stems from his own innate qualities and skills. As a record company executive, he has long understood the power of television to sell records. Indeed, in the days before *X Factor*, *American Idol* and the rest, he made a tidy living by identifying popular TV characters whose appeal could be exploited via records and CDs.

For instance, in the 1990s, Cowell was responsible for the release of two top-selling albums by a duo dubbed Robson and Jerome. Both actors, the duo appeared together in the popular TV series, *Soldier Soldier*. In one episode they gave an on-screen rendition of the Righteous Brothers song, 'Unchained Melody'. There was a huge response from viewers, prompting a hit-hungry Cowell to sign the pair. The result was a run of hit singles – starting with 'Unchained Melody' – and two best-selling albums. Cowell and record label BMG were laughing all the way to the bank.

But that was just the start. Although *X Factor/American Idol* style singing contests were by no means Cowell's invention, he has set about commercially exploiting the format, with an energy, inventiveness and talent for self-promotion that has left rivals standing in the background.

It's the self-promoting Cowell that the public know best. Since his first TV appearances on *Pop Idol*, he has earned a reputation for (depending on his mood) blunt speaking or downright rudeness, aimed at hopefuls who appear before the judging panels. Indeed, his catch phrase – also the title of his autobiography – is 'I Don't Mean To Be Rude But'.

His willingness to tell it like it is has served him well. When he appears on-screen on a talent show, Cowell is always the star. Yes, he generally appears with other successful and opinionated people, but it is Cowell's carefully honed opinions that viewers are waiting for.

But if Cowell was nothing more than a very rude man the shows wouldn't work. The role he inhabits with the consummate ease of a born showman is that of the music industry expert who knows talent (or the lack of it) when he sees it. And while he certainly seems prepared to quash the hopes of those less talented, he can be rich in praise for those with a singing style and charisma that he finds appealing.

And audiences have warmed to him. At times he may seem to come across as a pantomime villain but underlying Cowell's talent show appearances is a genuine quest to sort out the wheat from the chaff and find one or two people who have the talent to make a music business career. It's a high stakes game and one that makes Cowell and his business partners a lot of money.

THE MAN BEHIND THE BRAND

Simon Cowell was born in Brighton in October 1959 but the family moved to Elstree shortly afterwards.

Cowell had a relatively privileged upbringing in more ways than one. His father – Eric Cowell – had carved out a successful career as an estate agent and the family were comfortably off. And as he grew up in Elstree – a centre for UK film-making – Cowell was surrounded by affluence and glamour. The family home sat next to that of Gerry Blatner, the then head of Warner Brothers films in the UK, and the young man often came into contact with the great and the good of the international movie business. According to Cowell's unofficial biographer – Chas Newkey-Burden – the young man even got to spend time with Hollywood legend Bette Davis, sitting at her feet as she learned her scripts[3].

By all accounts, the family fitted in well with life in Elstree. Eric was comfortable with the showbiz elite and later – when Cowell was looking for a job – he was influential enough to secure him employment at record company EMI. Cowell's mother, Julie was equally at home. She came from a theatrical background – performing under the stage name Julie Brett – so the world of actors, actresses and show business impresarios was one she knew very well.

As a boy, Cowell spent time in the Warner Brothers studio, watching the actors and directors work. It was probably the perfect start in life for a young man who would ultimately become a major player in the entertainment industry. In the Cowell home and on the studio lots of Elstree all the building blocks were in place. He had first-hand experience of the glamour afforded by show business life and, in his father, he had a living, breathing example of what could be achieved through hard work and business acumen.

In the UK, Cowell was paid more than £6m in 2009 for his work on *X Factor*, while in the US Fox shelled out £20m for his services on *American Idol*.

Cowell demonstrated a certain amount of personal commercial acumen at an early age, starting a car cleaning business when he was eight years old. It's an experience common to many children. Realizing the limitations of pocket money, they look for ways of raising a bit of extra cash through paper rounds, odd jobs or cleaning the neighbours' cars. It's not necessarily an indicator of success in later life, but it provides a good grounding in the relationship between hard work and money.

And Cowell's mother was determined that the family's affluent lifestyle wouldn't give the young boy the spurious impression that the good things in life arrive pre-packaged. Speaking to the *Daily Mail* she revealed that she had made him work: 'I made them get all sorts of jobs … They didn't need to work, but I felt it was so important that they get out there and learn that money doesn't grow on trees.'[4]

If Cowell was industrious in pursuit of cash, he was much less eager to apply himself to academic work. By his own admission, Cowell hated school, with all the associated discipline and rules. After attending Radlett Preparatory School he was sent to Dover College, a private boarding school in Kent. Living away from home for the first time didn't improve Cowell's attitude and in academic terms at least, he didn't thrive. At times miserable and mostly rebellious he endured the experience of Dover College reluctantly and when he left at the age of sixteen he had just two O levels to call his own. 'I was like so bored [at school]', he told *Now* magazine in 2008, 'I don't like rules or discipline. So when someone said, "These are the best days of your life" I actually thought about jumping off a bridge.'[5]

Poor educational attainment is something that crops up a lot in the biographies of successful entrepreneurs and the movers and shakers of the business world. Sometimes the success in the 'real world' of building a business is a case of needs must. An individual who leaves school with very little in the way of qualifications will find many of the traditional pathways to an affluent lifestyle firmly blocked. Without a good brace of O and A levels you can forget about a cosy career in law, medicine or accountancy. Sometimes the only way forward is to start a business.

But an inability or unwillingness to settle down into schoolwork can also be an indicator of a certain personality type. School is about rules, discipline and the application of effort to a range of subjects that are less than engaging to young minds. While some buckle down and get on with it, others are simply too restless or rebellious to get with the programme. Or to put it another way, they are unwilling to bend to the will of the school authorities. It's a personality type that often lends itself to the entrepreneurial lifestyle.

Cowell appears to fit that profile. Inside and outside school he was known as a handful and even his loving mother Julie had her despairing moments. Despite this, she saw something important beneath the rebellious façade. She knew he was ambitious.

CAREER OPPORTUNITIES

In retrospect, we can see life falling neatly into place for Simon Cowell. A childhood spent in Britain's very own mini Tinseltown, a disregard for authority, a rebellious streak that saw him smoking in his early teens, a sense of ambition. As he grew older the rebellion and the ambition modulated into something more constructive – a determination to succeed while doing things his own way. It was a determination that took him from post-room boy at EMI records to music mogul with the world at his feet.

But that neat summation of Cowell's life comes courtesy of the 20/20 vision of hindsight. The truth is that while there is no shortage of successful people who leave school with little to show by way of qualifications – witness Jamie Oliver, Duncan Bannatyne and Richard Branson for example – life can be incredibly tough for those who don't acquire the safety net of O levels, A levels and degrees. When Cowell embarked on the world of work, no one could have known that his ultimate destiny was to achieve enormous financial success, media industry power and celebrity status.

He had several things in his favour, though. He certainly didn't lack self-confidence and a belief in his ability to succeed. Equally important, he had a strong family background from which to draw support. Indeed, it was Eric Cowell who got him his first job as junior employee in record company EMI's mail room. That post – lowly as it was – provided a starting point from which he could build a career.

But there were some hard times ahead. Cowell quit the post boy job only to return to EMI shortly afterwards, again with the help of his father. The new job was much more to his liking. Working as an artist and repertoire (A&R) man he was tasked with finding songs from the international company's US catalogue that would be suitable for British artists to perform.

As a record company executive, he has long understood the power of television to sell records.

Still restless, he quit EMI to join colleague Ellis Rich in the formation of an independent record label, E&S. The venture wasn't a success – at least as far as Cowell was concerned – so in 1985 the young man found a new role at Fanfare Records, a label set up by successful entertainment industry manager, Iain Burton.

It was with Fanfare that Cowell had his first real success. Having discovered and befriended teenage singer Sinitta, he found the song ('So Macho') that would take her to the top of the charts. Struggling to find a second hit for his protégé, he persuaded record producer Pete Waterman to work with him. Waterman was a key part of the legendary and highly successful songwriting and producing partnership Stock Aitkin and Waterman (SAW) and, under his tutelage, Cowell had more hits with Sinitta while building up a portfolio of other successful artists, including Gloria Gaynor.

But in 1992 things began to go wrong for Cowell. When the parent company ran into financial difficulties, Fanfare Records closed its doors. It was a bleak period. Faced with the double whammy of debts and no income, Cowell was forced to return to his parents' house where he lived temporarily.

Note the date. Cowell was born in 1959 and when Fanfare Records folded he was in his early thirties. Yes he'd had success, but the fruits of his labour – cars, houses, holidays – had been swept away by the failure of Fanfare. In many respects he was back to square one.

He bounced back. After Fanfare collapsed, the company's back catalogue of recorded music was bought by BMG – later Sony BMG – and Cowell was offered a job as an A&R consultant. It was a fruitful period. During the 1990s he signed a number of highly successful acts, including Westlife, Curiosity Killed the Cat, Sonia and Five and ultimately went on to set up his own S Records as part of the BMG stable.

He also emerged as an opportunistic hit maker with a special gift for record buyers who would be susceptible to novelty releases tailored to their interests. TV spin-offs were a particular specialty. Cowell would identify a programme with a strong fan base – often focused on children – and release records exploiting the popularity of the show. Records themed to the Teletubbies, Power Rangers and puppets Zig and Zag were among his successes. In a variation on that strategy, he released singles and an album exploiting the popularity of WWF wrestling. Looking to the adult audience, he had huge success with the aforementioned Robson and Jerome.

TV TIMES

It was to be a decade before Cowell made the transition from little known executive at BMG to star of *Pop Idol*, *American Idol*, *X Factor* and *Britain's Got Talent*.

The catalyst was Nigel Lythgoe, an experienced TV producer. He had just bought the rights to an Australian show dubbed *Popstars* and, in 2000, he sounded out Cowell on the possibility of appearing on the British version. Cowell turned it down.

That could have been the end of the story, but when the show turned out to be a success, Cowell got together with pop manager Simon Fuller – best known for his work with the Spice Girls – and began to formulate plans for a similar but better show. Nigel Lythgoe joined the negotiations and *Pop Idol* was born.

Like *Popstars* before and *X Factor* afterwards, *Pop Idol* was a talent contest designed to find pop performers who would go on to release hit records. Under the deal worked out by its creators, Simon Fuller's 19 Entertainment would own the show, while Cowell and BMG would release records by the winners. The die was cast.

Sitting in the judge's chair, Cowell quickly established himself as the star of *Pop Idol*, just as his presence dominates *X Factor* today. His screen presence didn't go unnoticed and when the show was sold to US TV as *American Idol*, the buyer, Fox Network asked Cowell to sit in judgment over American talent too. It was the beginning of Cowell's reign as an international man of media. The American audience loved his no-holds-barred approach and he became one of the most high profile figures in the US TV landscape.

Today, Cowell is continuing to surf the twin waves of celebrity and business success. In the UK he continues to dominate *X Factor* and *Britain's Got Talent* judging panels – the programmes themselves kingpins of the Saturday night TV schedules. Meanwhile his tenure with *American Idol* has come to an end and he is about to launch *X Factor* in the US.

RIDING THE CHANGES

Cowell is not a johnny-come-lately whiz kid. Now in his fifties, he didn't enjoy his current levels of success until relatively late in life. Nor is he a Branson-style lone gun. Much of his time in the record industry has been spent working for major labels such as Sony and BMG. Within those structures, he has often succeeded in securing a significant autonomy – not to mention a share of the profits – but he is in many respects an 'industry' man rather than an entrepreneur in the conventional sense.

And yet, within the context of the corporate world, he has succeeded in changing the landscape in which music is promoted and sold.

The music industry has been through some massive changes since the fateful day when Simon Cowell first stepped across the hallowed threshold of EMI records. That was in 1979 and the music industry was still in the grip of the punk/new wave revolution.

The furious energies of punk wouldn't survive long but the ethos of DIY pop that underpinned the movement would have a longer term influence. Through most of the 1960s and 1970s, the art of making records had been largely in the hands of industry giants such as CBS (now part of Sony) and EMI. The rules were simple. To become a successful band or musician you signed up to a major label, spent time in an expensive studio with a well known producer and produced a record that would be aggressively marketed and widely distributed. The industry was largely based in London.

Punk changed the rules. New labels sprung up, not just in London but all over the country. Some were cottage industry affairs, producing records for local sale. Others, such as Stiff (London) and Factory (Manchester) produced genuine hits and became influential players in the industry. Even after punk and new wave gave way to the New Romantic movement, the ethos of the independent (indie) record label continued.

It even entered the mainstream. Stock Aitkin and Waterman – the biggest hit-makers of the 1980s – were essentially an indie operation, handling songwriting, production and management under one roof. One by-product of this was an increasing willingness on the part of major record labels to allow quasi-independent labels and production houses to operate as part of the bigger group.

In its way, Cowell's career has reflected the influence of the indie movement on music industry business models. After a brief tenure at EMI he went on to work for two independent record companies – E&S and Fanfare. When he joined BMG he set up his own S label within the group. Today, after a renegotiation of his contract, Cowell's Syco companies are no longer 100% owned by Sony. Instead Syco is a 50% joint venture between Cowell and its one-time owner.

THE REVOLUTION WILL BE TELEVISED

A second revolution hit the industry in 1981 in the shape of a ground-breaking US cable channel – MTV.

The channel represented a new way of consuming music. Prior to the advent of multi-channel TV, radio was the primary conduit for promoting music to a mass audience. TV also played an important part in the process of hit-making, but it was largely a medium for acts which were already selling records in decent quantities. Radio was the key in terms of bringing new acts to public attention and the DJ was king.

MTV aped the format of radio. While music on the main television networks was confined to a few key shows, MTV played music videos through the day, just as radio stations played records. In other words, you could tune in at any time and watch videos or concert footage, all linked by Video Jockeys (VJs).

> **The fruits of his labour – cars, houses, and holidays – had been swept away by the failure of Fanfare. In many respects he was back to square one.**

Three decades on, MTV is perhaps not as influential as it used to be. For one thing, it has spawned its fair share of imitators and the electronic programme guides of satellite and cable services are packed with music stations aimed at a variety of demographic groups, from fans of urban music, through teenage pop to good old-fashioned guitar rock for the baby boomers.

Overall though, television has never been more important as a channel through which to promote music. It's a fragmented picture. Rolling format music TV of the type pioneered by MTV is devoured by committed music fans in their teens and early twenties, but it doesn't necessarily appeal to the broader TV audience that still likes to sit down in front of BBC or ITV for a mixed schedule of comedy, drama and light entertainment. *X Factor* and *Britain's Got Talent* are designed to appeal to that audience.

And here's the thing. The 14 million people who tune in to watch the *X Factor* finals every year represent a pretty broad church. Some of them are undoubtedly avid record buyers who know and care about music. Others buy maybe three or four records a year.

And among those viewers are casual and irregular consumers of CDs and downloads for whom Cowell's shows have come to define what pop music is. Much to the annoyance of critics, *X Factor* and *Got Talent* have become hugely influential in shaping the record buying habits of UK consumers.

He is a profoundly competitive man who is determined come out on top in any situation.

As such they have helped the industry buck an apparently unstoppable recent trend within the music industry – namely that of inexorably falling revenues.

Life was good for the music business in the 1980s and early 1990s. Supercharged by MTV, pop music flourished, while the phenomenon of baby boomers replacing their vinyl records with the shiny new CDs gave sales a further boost.

But since the dawn of the millennium there has been much weeping, wailing and gnashing of teeth in the face of sharp declines in sales figures, not just in the UK but around the world. For instance, according to figures published by the International Federation for the Phonographic Industry (IFPI), global record sales fell by 25% between 1999 and 2008. In monetary terms that meant the industry was selling $38.6bn worth of records at the end of the 1990s compared to $25bn in 2008. The rot didn't stop there. In 2009 there was a further 10% decline in all formats (CD, download, etc).

There are plenty of reasons for the decline. The industry itself is focused on illegal downloads and there's certainly plenty of evidence that a significant percentage of young people see no reason why they should pay for music when they can get it online for free. But perhaps as important is the fact that music CDs are no longer the only game in town when it comes to cheap home entertainment. DVDs, Blue Ray and video games across a range of formats are all competing for the consumer wallet, so it's not surprising that music sales are falling.

Against this picture, Cowell has presented himself as something of a saviour for the industry. For instance, talking to the *Daily Telegraph* he mounted a vigorous defence of *X Factor* and, by extension, his other shows, against accusations that they have been bad for the music industry: 'I would argue that when you've got over 13m people watching a music show on Saturday night, it is good for the music business.'[6]

There's some justification in his claim. While global record sales fell around the world in 2009, UK consumers bought more. As the *Independent* newspaper reported[7], UK sales rose 1.4%. The figures were boosted by sales of a few major artists including Michael Jackson (after his death), the Beatles (remastered CDs) and Cowell talent show alumnus Susan Boyle. It would be wrong to present Cowell as a man who is single-handedly saving the music business, but his TV shows undoubtedly shift records and get people into record shops at a time when the industry as a whole needs to maintain and raise interest in its products.

Arguably Cowell has also played an important role in bucking a second industry trend – the fragmentation of the TV audience. In the age of multi-channel TV and radio the attention of viewers is divided across hundreds of channels – analogue, digital and online. That inevitably means smaller viewing figures. Back in 1968, *The Morecambe and Wise Show* attracted 28 million UK viewers on Christmas Day. Such a figure would be unthinkable today.

But Cowell's 13-million-plus *X Factor* figures are pretty good. His carefully constructed shows are a textbook example of so-called appointment TV. These are the programmes that people gather round the water-cooler to discuss. And if you haven't watched them, or read about them online or in a newspaper, you're out of the conversation.

What's more, the audience for Cowell's show is engaged. Viewers vote and send e-mails to the spin-offs on digital channels. They are part of the drama.

SKILL SETS

So what is it about Cowell that has led to his success in this changing media landscape? Over the years, he has demonstrated a range of personal attributes and skills that have served him well in the music and entertainment industry.

Perhaps the greatest of these is pure determination to succeed. He is a profoundly competitive man who is determined to come out on top in any situation. You can see this on TV in the way that he dominates the judging panels on *X Factor*, *Britain's Got Talent* and *American Idol*. Off-screen his goal is not simply to secure hit records but to push his artists to the number one spot. In the UK, the Christmas number one is the Holy Grail and, thanks to *X Factor*, Cowell's record label has taken the top spot every year between 2005 and 2008. In 2009 there was hiccup. Thanks to a successful online campaign to get a non-Cowell act – Rage Against the Machine – to pole position, Joe McElderry had to wait until the new year to hit the top.

But determination to succeed is not in itself enough to sustain a career. Cowell is also very focused. In the context of the music industry, he wants hit records and the financial success they bring.

That doesn't necessarily mean great songs and singers. Cowell is clearly proud of the success of talent protégés such as *X Factor* winner Leona Lewis but he is unrepentant about his involvement in novelty hits by the likes of the stars of the World Wrestling Federation.

But securing those hits requires real insight. Cowell can spot talent and he has proved his ability to match songs with hit potential to artists with a broad public appeal. Equally, he is good at tailoring records for certain groups, such as wrestling fans or children who love the Teletubbies or Power Rangers.

Despite his very real self-belief, Cowell works closely with others and is prepared to learn from those with greater experience. This was particularly apparent in the 1980s, when he persisted in an ultimately successful attempt to persuade producer and songwriter Pete Waterman to work with him. Ostensibly Cowell wanted Pete Waterman's help on a follow-up hit for Sinitta, but his real goal was to learn as much as possible from a music industry supremo.

Above all, Cowell is prepared to innovate. From *Pop Idol* through to *X Factor* Cowell has honed a symbiotic relationship between music and TV. The talent shows boost ratings for the TV companies and in return his record label gets to sign artists that have been endorsed by millions of viewers ahead of their first records going on release.

In the rest of this book, we'll be looking in greater depth at Simon Cowell's business methods. As the following chapters make clear, he is not some flash in the pan who burst onto television screens from nowhere. The years he spent learning his industry from the ground up and defining his own audience played a crucial part in enabling him to take fame and influence that came through *X*

Factor and *Pop Idol*. But nor is he a corporate salary man who got lucky. He is an innovator and a leader with the drive and will to take a good idea and exploit it to the full. Some would say he is a maverick but he works effectively with partners, colleagues and artists. These are just some of the elements underpinning his success.

AT A GLANCE

EARLY LIFE

- Born 1959 in Brighton on the South Coast of England to Eric and Julie Cowell. The family – including Cowell's three half brothers – moved to Elstree shortly afterwards.
- Attended Radlett Preparatory School.
- Boarded at Dover College. Left at sixteen with two O Levels.
- 1979 – Joined EMI in the post room. Quit that particular job but after a short break rejoined the company in the publishing department.

EARLY CAREER

- Cowell left EMI to set up the record label E&S in the early 1980s with Ellis Rich.
- Joined Fanfare Records, a company set up by Iain Burton. During that time discovered teenage singer Sinitta and was responsible for developing her career. She scored her first hit with 'So Macho'.
- In 1984, Cowell met record producer and songwriter, Pete Waterman. Waterman, part of the Stock Aitkin and Waterman production team worked with Cowell on a second hit for Sinitta. The two men worked together on other projects, and Cowell sees Waterman as a mentor.
- 1989 – Fanfare Records folds under the weight of debts.

THE ROAD TO SUCCESS

- 1989 – Cowell joined BMG records as an A&R man. Formed S Records within the company. Has pop hits with Five and Westlife, Curiosity Killed the Cat and Sonia. Also has novelty hits aimed at fans of WWF wrestling, The Power Rangers, puppet duo Zig and Zag and the Teletubbies. One of his biggest successes was with Robson and Jerome, two actors riding high on the popularity of ITV's *Soldier, Soldier* series. They got a huge response when they sang 'Unchained Melody' in an episode of the series. Realizing the commercial potential, Cowell signed the duo and released two albums of pop standards.

TV

- In 2000, Cowell and Simon Fuller put together plans for *Pop Idol*, a knockout talent show aimed at finding successful recording artists.
- 2001 – ITV agrees to buy the show. Under the terms of the deal, Fuller will own the rights to the show while Cowell will sign the winning artist.
- Cowell sets up Syco records, which will operate as part of the Sony BMG group.
- 2001 – *Pop Idol* is pitched to US TV. Fox buys it.
- 2004 – Cowell launches *X Factor* on ITV.
- 2006 – *America's Got Talent* launches on NBC as a generalist talent show. *Britain's Got Talent* launches a year later. The *Got Talent* franchise is sold around the world.
- 2010 – Sony cedes its 100% control of Syco for a 50% share in a joint venture.

1
KNOW YOUR INDUSTRY

'I had to start at the bottom and climb very slowly to whatever you perceive to be the top. I'm glad I did it that way. I wouldn't have wanted any quick breaks.'[1]

– Simon Cowell

When Simon Cowell appeared on US television's venerable current affairs show *60 Minutes* in 2007, interviewer Anderson Cooper was anxious to establish what the English mogul actually did to earn his multimillion dollar income.

Cowell freely admitted that he had no musical talent in the conventional sense. He didn't sing, he strummed the guitar badly and he played no part in producing the hit records that had set him on the path to multimillionaire status. And when pressed by Cooper, he described his role in surprisingly modest terms.

'I take a guess at what's going to be popular,' he said. 'It's literally that.'[2]

Sounds easy, doesn't it? All you seem to need to make a fortune in the music industry is an instinctive ear for the kind of song that will persuade the record buying public to part with their hard-earned cash. Indeed, as Cowell went on to assert, when it comes to steering a record to its rightful home at the top of the charts, too much musical knowledge can be a dangerous thing. 'It's an advantage not knowing much about music because it means I follow my instincts,' he added.

Cowell's instincts are of course legendary. Since his discovery of teenage chart-topper Sinitta in the 1980s he has proved adept at finding artists and matching them up with hit songs. From mainstream pop, through to novelty records and even opera – fronted by singers with boy-band good looks – he's proved time and time again that he has the ability to spot the song that will sell. However, it's not simply a question of knowing a good tune when he hears it. His real gift is in spotting commercial potential.

But despite what Cowell likes to suggest, his success isn't entirely down to unerring instinct. In music industry terms, Cowell was a slow burner. While he certainly had hits in the 1980s and early 1990s, he didn't emerge as a major industry player until much later. Indeed, it wasn't until 2001 that *Music Week* magazine – the industry's trade paper – named him as an executive to watch.

Prior to that, Cowell had spent two decades learning the industry from the bottom up. His grounding in the machinations of the pop world meant he was fully ready to capitalize on the opportunities that flooded in when *Pop Idol* and *X Factor* catapulted him to global success.

FIND A NICHE

Cowell doesn't write songs or work with bands in the studio, but early on in his career he found a niche as an Artist and Repertoire (A&R) man.

The music industry has its own ecosystem of backroom professionals. These include songwriters, producers, recording engineers and managers. All of these people play vital and generally complementary roles in what Joni Mitchell called 'the star making machinery behind a popular song.'

In the centre of this ecosystem the A&R professional is there to hold it all together. Put simply, an A&R man (or woman) is there to spot and develop talent. When a budding hopeful sends a demo CD to a record label, it's the A&R team that will have first listen. They'll also be reading the music press – to find out who is up and coming – hanging out in clubs and music venues and generally doing anything they can to find tomorrow's stars.

Once an artist has been signed the work continues. In the world of mainstream pop, performers generally aren't encouraged to write their own material – unless they can demonstrate a clear talent in that direction – so the job of A&R is to find the song that suits the artist. Match the right performer to the right song and you have a decent chance of having a hit record. If you don't get the pairing right, then all the promotion in the world probably won't deliver a coveted place in the top twenty.

But it's not all about instinct. In music industry terms, Cowell was a slow burner ... he didn't emerge as a major industry player until much later.

That doesn't mean you have to find a great song. The trick is to find songs that a) fit the singer or band and b) strike some sort of chord with the record buying audience. It's an art rather than a science and, like it or not, Cowell is an artist of sorts.

But he also has a wealth of industry experience behind him. As far as the general public is concerned, the Cowell era began when *Pop Idol* and then *X Factor* catapulted him onto the Rich List while also establishing him first as a household name and latterly as a national treasure. But he spent the 1980s and 1990s learning the business. By the time he moved into TV he knew just about all there was to know about his particular branch of the pop music spectrum. He could tell if a song had hit potential. He could spot talent. Perhaps most importantly, he knew his audience and how to sell records to them via TV and the press. So when *Pop Idol* and *X Factor* came along, he was equipped with all the industry knowledge that enabled him to pick the winners of TV talent shows and market them to the world as recording stars.

GET YOUR FOOT IN THE DOOR

Cowell started at the bottom. Famously, he didn't do well at school, finding lessons boring. When he emerged from his private school – Dover College – to face the world of work, he had just two O levels to his name. He certainly wasn't in a position to step into a highly paid job.

In the months that followed, Cowell tried labouring – that lasted two days – and didn't make it past the interview stage when he applied for posts at Tesco and the Civil Service. He did, however, manage to get a temporary job as a runner at Elstree film studios.

In an alternative universe, this could have been Cowell's big break. The runner is the lowliest job in the film industry – essentially it involves running errands for just about everyone else on set – but it is seen as a foothold from which the ambitious can begin an ascent to the top. In this case the job provided only a temporary taste of the glamour of the industry. The contract came to an end after three months and Cowell was back in the job market.

That was when his career really began. Cowell's father – an estate agent – had connections with record company EMI and he managed to get his son a position in the company's mail room. If anything this was an even lowlier job than that of the runner and, according to Cowell's mother, the boy reacted to the offer of the position with a mixture of despondency and awareness that it could lead to greater things. Talking to the *Daily Mail* in 2007 she recalled him saying to her: 'This is just a stepping stone, Mum. I want more.'[3]

Arguably, a job in the mail room didn't really represent much of a beachhead in the music industry. Yes, Cowell was working for EMI, which was and is one of the world's biggest and most respected record label. But frankly, he was delivering mail. He could have been working for any big company in any industry.

By all accounts Cowell did his best to turn adversity to his advantage. According to biographer Chas Newkey-Burden[4], he tried to make contacts within the company. Delivering mail meant visiting every department within EMI, in theory at least, offering him the chance to rub shoulders with the great and the good and perhaps promote himself as an ambitious young man, anxious to progress and do great things.

The truth is, of course, that simply being within the four walls of an organization is not necessarily a passport to promotion. In a creative industry, few people are going to even notice the mail man, let alone single him out for fast tracking into a more rewarding post. Cowell was in a job that had no career path.

Cowell apparently realized that. He jumped ship after a few months to pursue a career in property. When that didn't work, he returned to EMI, this time in a position that was more to his liking.

More to the point, it was a job where he could begin to learn his trade. As a company, EMI is an exemplar of the UK's strength in the global entertainment market. Not only does it export British talent to the world, it also signs and nurtures artists from all over the globe.

Cowell's job, when he returned to the company, was to scour the overseas catalogue and match them with British artists. The idea was that he would sell the songs to artists who weren't necessarily signed to the label. It's probably fair to say that it wasn't the most coveted post within EMI but it was one that offered the ambitious Cowell an opportunity to make a name for himself.

He knew a good song. He could spot talent. But perhaps more importantly, he knew his audience and how to sell records to them via TV and the press.

If the first rule of working your way up through a company is finding a job with a career path, the second is to undertake your role with all the energy, enthusiasm and talent you can muster. Cowell embraced the challenge and proved adept at matching songs to artists. At the same time, he was immersed in music. He was getting a feel for the kind of intangible magic that makes a song work. He was learning to distinguish between the hits and the misses.

But if EMI offered Cowell the opportunity to build a long term career he wasn't minded to undertake a protracted apprenticeship. Had things gone well, the company could have given Cowell a thorough grounding in the music industry. It had a vast A&R operation with artists as diverse as Geri Halliwell (the former Spice Girl), the Red Hot Chilli Peppers and REM on its books. As such, it offered its A&R team the chance to work with a wide range of music from chirpy, manufactured pop to serious-minded rock.

And had he done well, EMI would doubtless have offered the young man a chance to rise through the corporate hierarchy to a senior position. It's a time-honoured route to success. You join a large organization and work within its structures and culture. In the early days, you'll be surrounded by people with much more experience than you. Formally or informally, they will be your mentors, teaching you about the industry and how it works. As the months and years pass, you'll assume increased responsibility and if you're very talented (and perhaps also lucky), you'll take your first steps on a promotion ladder that could take you right to the top.

TAKE A GAMBLE

There is, however, another way to learn an industry. Rather than sticking to one company for five, ten, twenty or thirty years, you move around and glean experience from a broad range of situations. You might even take the ultimate gamble and start your own company. This was the route taken by Cowell.

His first foray outside the corporate comfort was E&S music, a venture set up by Cowell himself and EMI colleague Ellis Rich in 1982.

The two men were at opposite ends of their careers. Cowell was, in industry terms, 'wet behind the ears'. Rich on the other hand had enjoyed a long career at EMI, working his way up through the ranks.

Rich began his career in music publishing at Feldman in 1963, a publisher that was later taken over by EMI. Unlike Cowell, he was very much a musician. A skilled pianist he himself spent time in the post room before progressing to a role transcribing the pop hits of the day into musical notation for publication as sheet music. Later he became International Manager at EMI, effectively Cowell's boss.

Thus, when Cowell agreed to work with Rich, he wasn't casting himself adrift from the music world. It was a gamble certainly, but if Cowell had youth and energy, Rich had almost twenty years of industry experience. He was someone that Cowell could learn from.

Many of the lessons learned were hard ones. E&S was set up at a time when independent labels and production companies were becoming the norm rather than the exception. There had always been independent operators but the DIY approach to music that characterized the punk and new wave era of the 1970s generated an explosion of small players aiming at niche markets. By the 1980s, the independent trend had spread to mainstream pop.

But signing and developing artists for the pop market is always going to be expensive and E&S was beset by funding problems when Cowell was on board. The glamour and kudos that came from running a music company didn't translate into sales. In this kind of situation there are two options. You hang on in there, hoping for the breakthrough that will move the business forward, or you decide to cut your losses and jump ship. That can be a tough call. When you've invested time, energy and money in a venture, it's often difficult to admit to yourself that the project is dead in the water. As a result, you stick with it for longer than you should, wasting more time, energy and money. On the other hand, if you jump ship too early, you might miss out on a deal or an opportunity that lies just over the horizon. There's no easy answer to the 'should I stay or should I go' dilemma. All you can really do is assess the situation and make a decision that you're going to stick with.

Cowell acted decisively, spending only a short time with E&S before quitting to take up a post with the newly formed Fanfare Records.

Ironically, E&S achieved some significant success after Cowell's departure. The company discovered chart-topping duo Mel and Kim and, buoyed by that success, Rich went on to found two successful music publishing operations, Supreme Songs and the Independent Music Group. Cowell, meanwhile, had Fanfare Records and he too was about to taste success.

BE PREPARED TO FIGHT YOUR SPACE

Fanfare Records was the brainchild of Iain Burton, an entertainment industry manager who had made his name guiding the career of choreographer Arlene Philips. These days Philips is probably best known – in the UK at least – as one-time judge on BBC Television's *Strictly Come Dancing*, but back in the 1970s and 1980s she was Britain's best known choreographer thanks to her work with dance troop, Hot Gossip. Hot Gossip shot to national fame through tightly disciplined and often provocative routines. Prior to their first appearance on national television no one had seen a dance troop quite as tightly drilled or as openly sexual. Philips became one of the hottest names in the entertainment world.

Burton had made his fortune managing Arlene Philips and had put some of his money into setting up Fanfare Records. He needed a partner with music industry and experience and Cowell got the job.

Fanfare Records represented a different kind of learning curve for Cowell. Unlike Ellis Rich, Burton was a manager rather than a music industry insider. Arguably, when it came to finding talent and good songs with hot potential, it was Cowell who had the music business experience.

But Cowell had to fight his space. Cowell's first real break into the heady world of music industry success came with the discovery of American teenager Sinitta Malone. Cowell was convinced she had hit potential and found the song which he believed could take her to the top of the charts. Meanwhile, Burton was reportedly thinking of closing down the Fanfare music operation to concentrate on other aspects of his business.

It's a situation that is probably more than familiar to anyone who has worked in an entrepreneurial start-up. When the company begins to trade you have a business plan outlining what you want to sell, how you will market it and what you expect to earn. Most business plans don't survive in their original form for more than a few months. Once a business leaves the drawing board and begins to trade, the realities of the marketplace begin to kick in. Some lines sell better than others. Costs multiply. Carefully laid plans don't work out. The upshot is that the owner takes another look at the plan – focuses on those aspects of the business that are most likely to deliver a return and jettisons the rest.

If the first rule of working your way up through a company is finding a job with a career path, the second is to do the job your doing with all the energy, enthusiasm and talent you can muster.

And in the case of Fanfare, had Burton gone ahead with his plan to close down the music operation, we might have heard no more of Simon Cowell.

In fact, Cowell won a reprieve for his project. He was given the go ahead to record Sinitta and, after three attempts, she achieved chart success with 'So Macho'. The song peaked at number two in the UK and ultimately sold something in the region of 1.5m copies.

What made this more impressive was that Cowell secured a hit on a £5,000 budget, a sum that would barely pay the monthly bar bills of some industry players. From the relative insecurity of an independent record label, he had been instrumental in steering a record into the charts. He would build on that experience to create more hits in his remaining years with Fanfare.

But to do this, he realized that he still had a lot to learn. Looking out at the music industry jungle, he knew there were much bigger and more successful beasts on the prowl and he wanted to follow in their footsteps.

LEARN FROM THE BEST

In the mid-1980s, few musical partnerships were more successful than Stock Aitkin and Waterman – aka SAW. The SAW songwriting and production partnership began in 1984 when the three men teamed up to produce Cyprus' entry for the Eurovision song contest. Hard on the heels of that project, they scored a breakthrough hit with Dead or Alive's 'You Spin Me Round' and followed this up producing a string of hits for girl group Bananarama.

But that was just the beginning. SAW really hit their stride when they applied the techniques of the assembly line to music production. Essentially, SAW took complete control of the music production process. They would write the songs, record them and select a singer. The artists whose names adorned the record sleeves often had very little input into the process other than to show up at the studio and record vocals on top of a pre-recorded track. On occasion the same backing track would be used to form the basis of more than one song.

This proved to be a highly efficient way of creating hit records. Artists were chosen on the basis of their looks, voices and overall appeal to the target audience of teens and early twenties. The deal was a simple one. SAW knew what they were doing in terms of songwriting and production and were equally adept at finding artists who could successfully front their creations. The acts they signed weren't exactly faceless or lacking in charisma but singers weren't expected to be creative. SAW would choose – and in most cases write – the songs that were released. Most artists had little say over the course of their careers.

On the business front, SAW would typically sign 'development deals' that would give the partnership pretty much total control over the careers of the singers they signed. They maximized revenues by retaining the publishing rights to songs recorded in their studios. This allowed them to earn revenue from, for example, the recording of a song by a different artist, or when used in a different context like an ad campaign, as well as from sales of the disc itself.

SAW had a reputation that extended way beyond industry insiders. While they certainly had big names on their books – Kylie Minogue being a case in point – the Stock Aitkin and Waterman sound had its own identity. Rather like Simon Cowell today, SAW were better known to the general public than some of the artists who fronted their creations.

By the mid-1980s, they were the British pop industry's most high profile players. Cowell was keen to not only harness their talents but also learn from their success.

There was a very good reason why Simon Cowell latched onto SAW – and in particular Pete Waterman. With a single Sinitta hit under his belt he wanted a follow up. Stock Aitkin and Waterman knew how to create hit records. They had the studio, the team, the skills and the track record. And while nothing in the music industry is certain, a SAW production was probably the nearest thing you could get to a cast iron guarantee of a chart-topping record.

Cowell reportedly pursued Waterman in a bid to persuade him to write and produce the follow up single for Sinitta. He was unsuccessful at first. As Cowell himself has acknowledged, the older man repeatedly rebuffed the young Turk's advance. However, demonstrating the persistence and self-confidence that has become part of Cowell's stock-in-trade, he continued to approach the producer with ideas for singles. Eventually, Waterman agreed to collaborate, writing and producing 'Toy Boy', Sinitta's second hit.

That in itself was all good. Sinitta and her mentor Cowell were no longer one-hit wonders and, after that initial collaboration, Waterman went on to work on more records for Fanfare. Later in the relationship, Waterman licensed the label to release a SAW greatest hits album.

But Cowell was getting something other than record sales and money from the relationship. It was a chance to learn the ropes of the music industry from someone at the top of his game.

It's hard to think of the hyperconfident Cowell worshipping at the feet of a music industry guru, but the younger man – not noted for suffering fools gladly – was clearly willing to learn from someone he liked and respected.

And, in retrospect, you can see Simon Cowell's approach to business mirroring that of his mentor. SAW were operating a hit factory. As the producers of the product they were in charge, mostly (if not always) providing the songs and sound while also managing their artists in terms of image, public appearances and media access. They assembled a talented team of engineers, stylists and marketing experts. At the end of the day, it was SAW who called the shots and not the artists on their roster.

Fast forward to the present day and Cowell has his own hit factory. Unlike SAW back in the 1980s, it has a new source of talent in the form of globally franchised TV shows, but the process of grooming and marketing a potential 'star' is very much the same. Once signed to Syco, artists are part of a hit-making machine, with Cowell and his team dictating the song, the look, the musical direction and the marketing plan. Everything is controlled and packaged to maximize the potential for a hit.

And you could argue that Cowell has long since taken the pop Svengali mantle from his old mentor. While he cheerfully acknowledges that Pete Waterman – still a friend – taught him how to make hit records and create a sustainable career, his own ability to use television both as a vehicle for promotion and a source for talent has made him one of the most powerful figures in the music industry.

Cowell's career with Fanfare Records ended when the parent company ran into financial problems. It was a watershed moment in the young man's career. Burdened with debts, he was forced to go back and live with his parents, eventually returning to the industry as an employee for BMG. But by then he'd served his apprenticeship. He was ready to become a serious player in his own right.

KNOW YOUR INDUSTRY

Prior to his successes on *Pop Idol*, Simon Cowell had spent more than two decades in the music industry, plying his trade as an artist and repertoire (A&R) man. He learned about his industry from the bottom up, starting with a major record company before branching out to run his own labels. This is how he gained his industry knowledge.

- **Find a niche.** Cowell admits he has little in the way of musical ability but he nonetheless found a niche within the record industry as a talent scout. He couldn't play, sing, produce recording sessions or write songs, but he was good at spotting hits, and this is where he staked out his territory for most of a long career. In all industries it's important to stick to what you're good at.
- **Get your foot in the door.** Emerging from school with only two O levels, Cowell's career options were limited and, while his father's connections got him a job with record company EMI, he started out in a lowly position. However, once he'd secured a job in the A&R department, he was determined to make the best of it. His ability to match songs with artists was noted and he was asked by one of his bosses, Ellis Rich, to establish a new independent music company. His experience demonstrates the importance of getting a break in your chosen industry and finding a niche that can offer a real career path.
- **Take a gamble.** Cowell joined Rich at E&S Records. Underfunded and initially unsuccessful it didn't fulfill Cowell's ambitions. However, it did give him a taste of working as a decision maker in a small firm. Although Cowell left E&S

a little more than a year after forming the partnership, he went on to his next venture with real experience of running a company. It was a gamble that didn't pay off in the short term but it set his career on a route that would ultimately lead to success.

- **Be prepared to fight your space.** Having joined another independent music company, Fanfare, Cowell had to fight to get the green light to release a record by protégé Sinitta. The single release, 'So Macho' was his first hit. With a success under his belt, he was in a strong position to produce more successful records for the company. The experience illustrates the importance of fighting for projects you believe in.

- **Learn from the best.** Despite his brash exterior, Cowell was more than happy to learn from those who were at the top of their game. Despite an initial rebuff, he persuaded producer Pete Waterman to work with Fanfare. The relationship not only produced hits, it allowed Cowell to watch a music industry 'genius' at work. Cowell has admitted he learned more from Waterman in two years than he would have done over a lifetime in the industry. Finding the right mentor can be an important step in a business career.

2
KNOW YOUR AUDIENCE

'He's got a wonderfully clear, intuitive mind which is undaunted by complexity. He doesn't let ideas get blown away because they might be slightly complicated and he has an unerring understanding of what ordinary people want.'[1]

– Tim Bowen, former SONY BMG executive on Cowell

S imon Cowell has a single goal – to sell enough CDs and downloads to propel his artists to the top of record industry sales charts in Britain and around the world. By his own admission, he is not much interested in critical acclaim and you're unlikely to find him engaging in long conversations about artistic merit. The success of a record released by the Cowell stable is judged by one thing only – whether or not it's a hit. A great record that nonetheless fails to make it to the higher reaches of the charts is a failure. Pure and simple.

Profiled on *60 Minutes* Cowell made it clear that his aim was to sell to a mass market rather than an elite few. 'A three-star Michelin chef probably looks at McDonald's and says that's terrible,' he told reporter Anderson Cooper. 'I'd rather be McDonald's than the three-star Michelin chef.'[2]

It's an approach that doesn't endear him to music critics. When the *New Musical Express* (*NME*) ran an interview with Cowell, editor Kris Murrison described *X Factor* as 'lightweight populist drivel' and Cowell himself as a 'money machine, laughing all the way to the bank.'[3]

Cowell was unrepentant. In his view, his TV shows were a force for good in the music industry, in that they drove record sales at a time when the music industry as a whole was watching its revenues decline. 'What I would argue in my defence is that shows like *Britain's Got Talent* and *The X Factor* have actually got people more interested in music again … We haven't seen this kind of uplift in years,' he told *NME*.[4]

One of the secrets behind Cowell's phenomenal success, as we saw in the first chapter, lies in his knowledge of the record industry, working with some of the industry's most successful management and production teams and learning all there was to know about marketing. He is also famously competitive, always aiming for the number one spot when he releases a record on his label.

But there is another important factor to consider. Much of Cowell's success has been built on an understanding of that all-important mass audience. Beyond the communities of dyed-in-the-wool, indie rock, hip hop, soul, grunge or metal fans there's a much larger group of people who buy a few records every year, often on a whim. It's a diffuse group. Some will respond to novelty records, others are partial to a big power ballad or a killer dance track and some respond to the nostalgic pool of songs from the 1950s or 1960s. Throughout his career, Cowell has demonstrated an understanding of this vast audience of casual music buyers.

The question is, where did this understanding come from?

KNOW WHO YOU ARE SELLING TO

All consumer markets can be broken down into segments. Take something as apparently ubiquitous as handbags. On the face of it, a handbag manufacturer is potentially addressing the entire female population. The reality is much more complicated. Within that overall group of buyers there will be huge variations. Some will be prepared to pay hundreds or thousands of pounds for designer creations while others will be content with something from Top Shop or Hollinger. And within those price points, you can break the market down further in terms of the age, class, peer group and socio-economic grouping of the potential buyer.

And from a marketing point of view, it's vital to know who a particular product is likely to appeal to. If your target market is teenage girls with relative low income in socio-economic groups C/D then you'll have to tailor any advertising and marketing campaigning to that particular segment. It's not simply a case of sending out the right marketing message, you have to understand the behaviour of your target consumers. Where do they go for entertainment? What media do they use (magazines, TV, internet sites, etc)? What are their cultural reference points? Unless you know where to find your audience, you won't be able to market to them effectively.

That principle applies in spades to the business of selling records. Walk into a branch of HMV on a busy Saturday and you'll find all human life gathering around the CD racks. From teenagers kitted out in the latest gear from Urban Outfitters or Jack Wills to pram-pushing dads and the occasional trendy pensioner, the store will be full of a diverse array of people. Each of them will be expressing their individuality or their place in a peer group through the records they buy.

Much of the segmentation in the music market is tribal or genre related. There are still plenty of music buyers who focus on a particular type of music, be it dance, grime, indie, folk or country.

That kind of tribalism makes it fairly easy to market artists through specialist publications and radio stations. For instance, if you want to break a new Indie band you get them an interview or a review in *NME* and send their records to radio DJs and producers who are known to play that type of music.

There are also demographic segments. Back in the 1980s the majority of records and CDs were bought by young people in their teens and early twenties. Today, it is adults in their mid-thirties and forties that account for the bulk of sales. Indeed, back in the 1990s the

British music industry identified '50 quid bloke' as its saviour. This was a music and movie obsessed middle-aged man who popped into HMV or the now defunct Virgin Megastores on a Saturday to spend a healthy wedge of cash – £50 on average – on CDs and DVDs. His one goal in life was to build a better music and movie library than his mates while reliving the glories of his youth.

> '… shows like *Britain's Got Talent* and *X Factor* have actually got people more interested in music again …'[4]
> **Simon Cowell**

Committed record buyers in their middle years are pretty easy to reach too. They probably don't listen to the radio as much as their younger counterparts, but they are well served for magazines. In the UK, magazines such as *Q*, *Mojo*, *Uncut* and *The Word* have done very nicely by catering to the needs of ageing music fans, often with diverse and eclectic tastes.

Cowell has defined his own target market – the aforementioned punter who buys three or four records a year – the silent majority who may not know (or care) much about music and yet have the power to deliver a Christmas number one single or a top-selling album.

These are the people who rush out to the shops to buy the first record from the winner of *X Factor*, *American Idol* or *Britain's Got Talent*. Without them Cowell's bank balance would be much smaller.

Let's take a closer look at the Cowell audience as it stands today. Given that his commercial interests are focused on the *X Factor* and *Got Talent* franchises, it's fair to assume that the record buying audience he has in mind broadly aligns with the audience of those shows.

For instance, not everyone who watches *X Factor* is going to do the decent thing and buy the associated records. A lot of people tune in to laugh at the open auditions or soak up the drama of the knockout phase while remaining largely unmoved by the subsequent recorded output of the winners.

But speaking to *Music Week* magazine in 2006, Cowell identified a key group of consumers – women over thirty with middle-of-the-road tastes – who could be mobilized by the show. They don't consume much music, but if they see something they like they will buy.

Cowell's shows provide an opportunity to focus their buying power on just a few records. Compare and contrast with '50 quid bloke'. There are millions of these little fellows filling their HMV shopping baskets every weekend, but here's the thing – they're buying records by a wide range of artists, so the spend is fragmented. Cowell's audience spend much less, but he's learned how to leverage their buying power to his products. A very neat trick.

So how exactly has he done that? Well, since the 1990s, Cowell has increasingly looked outside the music industry to find acts with proven popularity that could be used to drive music sales.

FOLLOW THE MONEY

If your goal is to tap into the mainstream pop market, you study the charts, take note of what sells and give the people what they want.

That's a tried and tested strategy. At any given time, record companies can see a range of genres that sell well to particular audiences.

So if chart positions one to thirty are neatly carved up between R&B, grime, hip hop, boy bands, girl bands and guitar driven indie, they hire A&R staff who understand those genres and sign more of the same.

And when Cowell had his first hit records with Sinitta, there was no great science behind his approach. He had the raw materials for a pop hit – a good looking singer with a decent voice and enough teen charisma to carry the day – and once he found the right song in the shape of 'So Macho' it was a case of taking a punt.

It was an educated punt, of course. As an A&R man, Cowell was well versed in the mainstream pop market of the day. He could see what was selling, he understood the pop genres and the production values of the time and he had sufficient faith in his own judgment to back his singer with £5000 of Fanfare Record's cash.

Cowell has defined his own target market – the aforementioned punter who buys three or four records a year – the silent majority who may not know (or care) much about music …

Cowell went on to have more success with Sinitta but it wasn't until the 1990s that he really began to hit his stride as a music mogul and by then he had hit on an arguably more efficient – and some would say ruthless – formula for creating hit records. He would look outside music to other branches of the entertainment world and identify artists or characters whose popularity could be exploited on record.

The first manifestation of this strategy came in the unlikely and undeniably beefy form of WWF Wrestlers.

If wrestling lacks the brutal appeal and gladiatorial credibility of boxing, it makes up for it in sheer showmanship. Wrestling has always been a sport for big characters who are skilled at blending their undoubted strength and athletic skills with pure theatre. It has its heroes and its pantomime villains and an appeal that stretches from grannies to children and teenagers. And when the big names of wrestling tour together, tickets fly out the door. It was the ability of World Wrestling Federation (WWF) events to put considerable numbers of bums on seats that first attracted the attention of Cowell.

The sales figures for WWF events in the UK intrigued him. Tickets – around 80,000 of them – for the organization's Summerslam at Wembley stadium in 1992 had sold out within 20 minutes. By implication that meant there were at least 80,000 committed wrestling fans who might be persuaded to buy a record release featuring their heroes.

The result of Cowell's brainwave was two chart singles – 'SlamJam' and 'Wrestlemania' – which peaked at 4 and 14 respectively. An album was also released both in Britain and the US.

The WWF wrestlers had form when it came to making music, having previously released two albums largely comprised of novelty songs. But under Cowell's stewardship, the songwriting and production was put into the more than capable hands of Stock Aitkin and Waterman. What they produced was a mix of their own dance oriented production techniques, sung vocals by professional singers and spoken contributions from the wrestlers. On the face of it, not a mix that you would automatically expect to set the charts alight but in a limited way, it did.

Perhaps more importantly, Cowell had latched on to a new route to market. Rather than simply putting out a record and hoping that it would get sufficient radio play and column inches to stimulate sales, he was aiming at a niche audience of consumers who were already fans of the characters in question. OK, so they weren't necessarily fans of the WWF stars as singers but they were already buying other forms of merchandise, so why not a single or an album? It was a strategy that Cowell would hone in the years to follow.

GIVE YOUR AUDIENCE WHAT THEY WANT

Witness his decision to home in on actors Robson Green and Jerome Flynn, co-stars of the 1990s drama series *Soldier Soldier*.

Focusing on the lives of a group of British soldiers, *Soldier Soldier* was a seriously popular show that ran for seven series between 1991 and 1996. By 1994 its viewing figures had climbed above 16 million, a figure that suggested around 65% of the viewing population were tuning in.

Cowell's eureka moment followed episode 9 of Series 4 when the onscreen friends Garvey and Tucker dueted on 'Unchained Melody', a 1965 hit for the Righteous Brothers. It was a performance that stirred a section of the ITV audience to write and call to ask the television company whether it was possible to purchase a recorded version of the song. Meanwhile, record shops were reportedly deluged by requests to buy the recording. At that point, it wasn't available.

Cowell sensed a ready-made audience. After all here was a performance that was manifestly being endorsed by a section of the public who appeared more than ready to buy a recorded version. With thousands of people making inquiries, sales were more or less guaranteed.

Cowell reportedly pursued the two actors for some time before persuading them to sign a record contract. Despite an initial and firmly expressed reluctance on their part, Cowell persisted and eventually got them into a studio to record a version of 'Unchained Melody', plus two albums that went on to sell around 7 million in total.

This was a long way away from the mainstream pop of Sinitta or the strange amalgam of talent that collaborated on the WWF records. The name of the game with Robson and Jerome was a collection of middlebrow pop standards that would push the buttons of the same viewers who wanted to buy 'Unchained Melody'.

So, in addition to that trademark song, the first album featured a mix of nostalgia tinged tracks, including 'Daydream Believer' (made famous by the Monkees), 'The Sun Ain't Gonna Shine Any More' and 'Up on the Roof'. In keeping with the project's military connections, the album also included 'There'll be Bluebirds Over the White Cliffs of Dover' – wartime diva Vera Lynn's best known song.

Looking over the tracklist as a whole, you won't find anything imaginative or ground breaking in the choice of numbers, but that wasn't the point. Fans of *Soldier Soldier* had already made clear what they wanted from Robson and Jerome – namely well known, singalong standards. Cowell made sure the audience got exactly what they wanted: karaoke favourites performed by a couple of actors who were fast on their way to becoming national treasures.

Cowell's adoption of television as a kind of market research tool didn't stop with Robson and Jerome. During the 1990s, he was also responsible for hit records themed around popular TV characters such as the Teletubbies, children's puppets Zig & Zag and the

Mighty Morphin Power Rangers. The formula was simple. Identify an audience associated with a popular show and put out records designed to appeal to those consumers.

INVOLVE THE MARKET

Few have taken music's relationship with television as far as Cowell. Through his involvement in *Pop Idol* and his stewardship of the all conquering *X Factor*, he has used the format of the television-talent-show-cum-singing-contest to find artists with the potential for success while simultaneously building an audience with a stake in that success.

Think of it this way. When a record producer takes a popular format such as WWF wrestling and fashions a record, there is no guarantee of success. Yes, the producer can certainly see that wrestling has a huge audience, but the question of whether that particular legion of fans will buy a spin-off record can only be answered when the discs arrive in the shops. It's a punt.

The same is true of singing TV stars. The reaction of *Soldier Soldier* viewers to their on-screen rendition of 'Unchained Melody' certainly suggested very strongly that there might well be a hit in the pipeline, but there could be no certainty.

But with *Pop Idol* and *X Factor*, the process of creating a hit record has become a matter of interactive market research over a period of weeks.

The broad format for these shows is well known. Thousands of people are auditioned to take part in the show. As the series progresses, the numbers are whittled down – first by the team of entertainment industry judges and in the final stages, by the public through telephone votes.

From a marketing point of view, the beauty of this system is that the public are intimately involved in selecting the artist who will go on to sign a record contract. *X Factor* – just like *Pop Idol* before it – is adept at creating stories around the hopeful contestants. There are mothers from one-parent families doing it for their kids, club singers in their thirties grasping a last chance at fame, and star-struck teenagers looking for a way to escape the mundanity of office or factory work.

While the winner walks away with a record deal and a near-certain top twenty hit, the losers mostly end up with nothing.

And the stakes are massively high. While the winner walks away with a record deal and a near-certain top twenty hit, the losers mostly end up with nothing. As the contestants are filtered, clear favourites emerge via the telephone voting systems. And by the time the victor is announced, millions of people have already committed themselves to the winning act. When the downloads and CDs go on sale, a large proportion of them will underline that commitment by reaching for their cash or credit cards.

As we'll see in a later chapter, harnessing the power of the crowd in this way requires a huge amount of careful management on the part of the TV companies and producers and Cowell has proved the supreme showman. At root, however, it's a simple principle. You get to know your audience by involving them in the A&R process. By voting for individuals, the viewers help create the stars and once the show is over, the same viewers – or a large percentage of them – buy the product. A glance at the hit-making achievement of these shows demonstrates their power to shift units.

Launched in 2002 and featuring Cowell as a judge, *Pop Idol*'s first final featured a showdown between Gareth Gates and Will Young. Both went on to secure long-term careers under the wing of BMG Records.

Fast forward to *X Factor*, and the hit machine keeps on running. The show's first winner, Steve Brookstein, had a number one hit and a best-selling album before sinking into obscurity, and Series 2 resulted in a number one single from a victorious Shayne Ward. In Series 3, *X Factor* struck true gold in the form of Leona Lewis.

Lewis – along with Will Young and Gareth Gates – provides demonstrable proof that the TV talent show format can produce artists with bankable long-term futures. On hearing that she'd won the 2006 final, Cowell said simply: 'I think she's one of the best singers we've seen in this country for a long, long time.'

Lewis's first album *Spirit* sold one million copies in the UK while 'Bleeding Love', the first single taken from the collection, hit the number one spot and hung on there for seven weeks. Perhaps just as important as the sales, Leona Lewis had artistic credibility. Often compared to soul divas such as Whitney Huston, she had respect as a singer and even managed to crack the difficult US market. 'Bleeding Love'was the first US number one by a British artist since 1987 and it launched a genuinely international career.

It would be wrong to suggest that Cowell's career has been entirely dependent on novelty records, TV spin-offs and talent shows. Certainly, that's where his fame and much of his wealth has come from, but he has also continued to work with and develop artists in the conventional way.

These include boy bands Five and Westlife, acts that had to be broken in the conventional way through radio play and magazines. And if those acts suggested a teen bias, his development Il Divo, a group of opera singers with boy band looks, suggested he was equally happy addressing older demographics.

However, it is Cowell's increasingly successful use of television that has marked him out not just as a successful label boss but as someone who is prepared to experiment with new ways of marketing music. His early experiments with TV as a marketing channel were relatively unsophisticated. He was certainly adept at making records based on the appeal of popular television characters, but he wasn't a pioneer in that regard. The TV-themed novelty record had been a feature of charts in the UK and beyond for many years prior to Cowell arriving on the scene.

But with *Pop Idol* and then *X Factor* Cowell entered a different league. He was not only getting to know his audience by studying viewing habits, but he became intimately involved with them through taking part in the same process of selection. In addition to phone votes, the audience feedback from a programme like *X Factor* is huge. Viewers/record buyers text the show, write blogs, leave comments on the production company website. It is a truly interactive process and one that makes the A&R man's job of giving the public what they want a whole lot easier.

KNOW YOUR AUDIENCE

Understanding the market is the key to successful marketing. Like any consumer market, the audience for music can be broken down into segments. Through his years in the industry, Cowell understands how the pop market breaks down and he is skilled at making records aimed at particular groups.

- **Know who you are selling to.** Pop music is famous for its tribal groupings – record buyers who focus on particular genres such as indie rock, adult oriented rock, metal, hip hop, R&B or dance. Fans of these genres can be reached through specialist magazines, websites and radio shows. Cowell is very aware of music's tribe but increasingly he is focused on a mass audience of consumers who perhaps buy three or four records a year. His skill is in identifying ways and means to mobilize this audience to buying his products.
- **Follow the money.** One technique that he has employed with great success is looking beyond music at other areas of the entertainment industry which have built a fan base with money to spend. For instance, one of his early successes with BMG was an album of songs featuring World Wrestling Federation stars. Tickets for WWF sold rapidly, as did the associated merchandise, prompting Cowell to suppose that wrestling themed music would also have an appeal. He was right. It's an illustration of the marketing rule that in order to sell to an audience you need to study their habits and the products they're already buying.

- **Give your audience what they want.** Cowell has also cashed in on the popularity of TV programmes and stars. Arguably his biggest success was with Robson Green and Jerome Flynn, stars of the 1990s TV series *Soldier Soldier*. A song performed by the actors as part of the drama series got a huge response, and thousands of people asked if a recorded version of the tune was available. This was a clear indication of demand and once signed by Cowell, Robson and Jerome went on to have two hit albums. It's an illustration of how sales success is often based not on a hunch but on a clearly defined appetite for the product.

- **Involve the market.** Cowell went on to use TV as a means to spot and filter talent. Talent shows such as *Britain's Got Talent* and *X Factor* involve the audience in selecting a winner from an initial cast of thousands. As the hopefuls are filtered through phone votes, viewers become closely engaged with the contestants. By the time the contest is over, millions of viewers have committed themselves to supporting the winning contestant. Many will go on to buy the subsequent record release. As winners are contracted to sign with Cowell's record label, he has secured himself a stream of new talent that already has public support. The interactive nature of the shows means Cowell and his audience are involved in the same process of selecting artists. By involving the audience he has become much closer to them.

3

HARNESS THE POWER
OF THE CROWD

'Crowdsourcing is companies taking a job that would normally be done by employees and outsourcing it in an open call to an undefined group of people.'[1]

– Jeff Howe, contributing editor,
Wired Magazine

The success of Cowell's *X Factor* raises an intriguing question. Here we have a man who has spent around 30 years in the music industry, spotting, developing and nurturing talent. As an artist and repertoire (A&R) man his role was to find artists and match them with songs that would appeal to a proportion of the record buying public.

But since the early noughties, his biggest successes have been secured through the participation of TV audiences around the world. Rather than spending his days sifting through piles of demo CDs sent in by hopeful stars in the making, he has discovered the stars of the future through televised talent contests and telephone votes. On the face of it at least, the winners of *X Factor*, *Britain's Got Talent* and *Pop Idol* have been chosen by the public, not by Cowell.

So the question is: has Cowell done himself out of a job? Has he ceded the process of finding big-selling mainstream pop artists to viewers of Saturday night TV shows?

Well the first thing that has to be said is that if Cowell has made himself redundant as a conventional A&R man, he has found a bigger and more lucrative role as the ringmaster of a complex process that brings together wannabe pop singers with the consumers who may one day buy their records. If the process is to work, it has to be compelling enough for those consumers to tune in and (most importantly) vote, week after week after week. And while Cowell didn't invent the idea of the interactive TV talent show, he is currently its most successful exponent.

So how does he make it work?

MAKE THE PUBLIC WORK FOR YOU

Talent shows have been a staple component of TV schedules since the early days of the medium and they have proved effective at discovering and promoting bankable entertainers.

In Britain, the granddaddy of them all was *Opportunity Knocks*. Launched in 1956 it was a show hosted by light entertainment stalwart Hughie Green and featured a range of acts from singers and musicians, through comedians to bodybuilders. By today's standards, *Opportunity Knocks* was cheesy in the extreme but, at least, it had some of the components of the modern talent show in place.

For one thing, the winners were selected by the public through a mixture of a 'clapometer' to measure the reaction of the live audience and postal votes. It's perhaps best remembered for slightly odd acts, such as bodybuilders flexing their muscles to music, but it also produced winners with enough firepower to secure hit records and television careers. Singer Mary Hopkins was among its discoveries.

Cowell himself was a fan of *New Faces*, a sharper talent show that was on UK television in the 1970s and 1980s. Like *Opportunity Knocks* it was a generalist show, not focused on any particular entertainment genre, but it differed from its predecessor in that winners were selected by a panel of judges.

Viewers of *X Factor* would find the judging panel strangely familiar. In amongst the line up of TV and radio presenters and light entertainment stars of the past and present, you would find record producer Mickie Most, musician and composer Tony Hatch and acerbic pundit Clive James. Marks were awarded out of ten across

Talent shows were an early manifestation of a phenomenon that was supposedly born in the internet age – crowdsourcing.

a series of categories, giving the judges ample opportunity to demonstrate either their generosity of spirit or hard professional realism. Tony Hatch famously gave one performer a zero, a move that saw him donning the mantle of Mr Mean for a time at least.

New Faces also succeeded in discovering viable talent and some of its alumni – notably Lenny Henry, Victoria Wood and the Chuckle Brothers are still pretty much at the top of their respective career trees today. On the music front, singer Patti Boulaye was the only contestant to achieve maximum points. Her reward was a long and successful career.

Talent shows were an early manifestation of a phenomenon that was supposedly born in the internet age – crowdsourcing.

In essence, crowdsourcing is the art of handing over a function that would normally be handled by employees within a company to a huge, unpaid workforce – namely the crowds.

In recent years, organizations have been using the crowd to perform a diverse range of tasks. In the software industry, companies routinely ask members of the public to test 'beta' versions of their new products to detect bugs before an official release. Scientists have used the internet to harness the processing power of millions of individual computers to help with scientific projects such as the search for intelligent life in space or research into new drugs. Online publishers encourage members of the public to supply videos, articles and blogs to fill up their sites. Marketers gather information on customer preferences and consumer trends through careful study of social networks and internet usage.

All of these are examples of how the wisdom, knowledge and energy of the masses can be leveraged by organizations to carry out tasks or hone products.

Perhaps inadvertently, Simon Cowell has tapped into the crowdsourcing phenomenon.

By combining elements of *New Faces* and *Opportunity Knocks* and tying them up with the techniques of modern television he has raised crowdsourcing as a market research and marketing tool into a fine art.

But – and this is a very big but – the magic formulae that have made *X Factor* and the various *Got Talent* franchises around the world into successful money-making machines required careful development and nurturing. Cowell's brainchildren are successful because he understands – or has come to understand – the key elements of successful, engaging TV. He also understands how to turn the popularity of his shows into hard cash. In doing so, he has made his own fortune while significantly swelling the coffers of Sony.

INCENTIVIZE THE AUDIENCE

The secret of crowdsourcing success is giving the audience a reason to take part. After all, people are busy – they have lives. If you want them to feed work or information back to your organization, you have to give them a good reason.

Sometimes the motivation is altruism. When scientists ask members of the public to download software that will contribute to an ongoing piece of research, with thousands of participating computers adding much needed processing power, the driver for most people will be the opportunity to help out in a valuable study.

On the other hand, the attraction may be financial. Whether contributing blogs to an online magazine or photos to an internet library, amateur writers and photographers are increasingly finding that the crowdsource model offers opportunities for payment. That might be direct payment – for instance, when an online picture library sells a photograph – or a share in advertising revenue.

More commonly, crowdsourcing projects work because they provide their audience with a means to make their voices heard. They can post blogs, upload videos to YouTube, or take part in ongoing market research.

In Simon Cowell's particular corner of the crowdsourcing universe the ability to vote – to make your voice heard – is certainly an important part of the equation, but that certainly isn't enough on its own. *X Factor* depends on a significant number of people committing time every week. If the show is to work, a critical mass of people have to follow the narrative of the various singers and artistes as they are whittled down and voted out in the journey towards the grand finale. As the show progresses, each regular viewer will identify favourites, see those favourites knocked out and switch their allegiance to others. Over the weeks, the non-committed will become committed until the time comes to cast the all important vote in the final.

In terms of revenue, *X Factor* serves at least three commercial purposes. Firstly, it maximizes the potential for record sales when the competition is over and the winner releases his or her first CD. Secondly it maximizes phone vote revenues. And thirdly, healthy audiences right through the series ensure that advertisers pay a

premium price for their slots. The same principles apply to *Britain's Got Talent*, *American Idol* and the various versions of those shows that are currently aired around the world.

ACT AS RINGMASTER

During his time as judge on *Pop Idol* and its US counterpart *American Idol*, Cowell demonstrated his ability to create memorable television moments. It was a talent that he developed and turned into a fine art when he began to produce talent shows in his own right, with *X Factor* and *Britain's Got Talent*.

On the face of it, much of the appeal of the above shows has been Cowell's near legendary rudeness but when you look beneath the surface of the shows there is a lot more going on. Each series has its own narrative arc as characters emerge, compete and bow out and, within that progression, its own dramas as judges and contestants clash. Cowell is far more than a judge with an acid tongue. Aided and abetted by his producers and fellow judges, he is a choreographer. A ringmaster.

But what does that mean in practice?

Well if we take *X Factor* as our starting point, we can see Cowell's hand at work in just about every aspect of the show. It's there in the way the contestants are presented. In the early stages of a series what we get is more or less what we see. Through the open audition stage – latterly in front of a live audience – hopeful contestants take the stage without the benefit of TV company grooming or priming. When they open their mouths to sing, they have no back story and the reaction of the judges and the audience depends purely on their performance. Or so it seems.

There is a certain amount of TV artifice. Those who appear on the 'open auditions' are in fact vetted before they go in front of the cameras and not everybody gets their moment in the television sun.

On the face of it, the vetting process should weed out the really poor performers, leaving a rump of decent singers who can at the very least hold a tune, but frankly that wouldn't be any fun. The skewering of the talentless and delusional in the 'open' audition stages has become part of the *X Factor*'s DNA. To those who watch the early stages of the show, much of the appeal lies in laughing or cringing as the hilariously hopeless make their bid for stardom. And when the minority of talented singers do take to the stage, their quality is all the more apparent. Put simply, they stand out against the dross.

X Factor depends on a significant number of people committing time every week. If the show is to work, a critical mass of people have to follow the narrative of the various singers and artistes as they are whittled down and voted out in the journey towards the grand finale.

Meanwhile, the presence of so many bad entertainers throws the spotlight on the real stars of the show – the judges. The mainstay is Cowell himself. If a singer is good, he'll lavish praise. If the performance is poor or simply mediocre, you can almost feel the anticipation as the audience waits for the savage, perfectly worded put down. Cowell seldom disappoints.

But if *X Factor* was simply the Cowell show it wouldn't work. Much of the creative tension revolves around the often tense relationship between the judges. Cowell's main foil is Louis Walsh, the Irish pop impresario who discovered and brought boy band Westlife to Cowell's attention. Walsh's understanding of mainstream pop and its audience is certainly equal to Cowell's. Both men have an unarguable track record when it comes to pushing their artists and they often disagree about the contestants who come under their scrutiny. Mostly those disagreements are good natured but Walsh and Cowell have had more than their fair share of ill-tempered exchanges.

In the early days of *X Factor*, Cowell and Walsh were joined on screen by Sharon Osbourne. As the wife of Black Sabbath singer Ozzy Osbourne, she was a little known figure until an MTV reality TV show projected her to cult fame. On *X Factor* she was seen as warmer than Cowell but equally mercurial. A bad singer could expect no mercy.

The Cowell/Walsh/Osbourne partnership made headlines and pushed up viewing figures but there was only one person in charge. As the decision maker, Cowell was (and is) exercising his right to shake things up. At one point, Walsh left the show and was subsequently reinstated. And at the end of Series 4 Cowell brought in a new judge, singer Danni Minogue, a move that led directly to Osbourne's departure. In a statement quoted in the *Daily Telegraph*, she said: 'I didn't enjoy working with her at all and the prospect of spending six months sitting next to her, I thought "my life is better than that".'[2]

So that was life on the *X Factor* judging panel. Bust ups between Walsh and Cowell, a walk out by Sharon Osbourne and, famously, the departure and return of Walsh. It was the kind of drama beloved by tabloid newspapers in the UK. The spats and fall outs between the *X Factor* judges have become a staple of the gossip and entertainment pages. That in turn was a guarantee that *X Factor* would always be in the headlines.

KEEP THE FORMULA FRESH

Cowell has always been aware of the importance of the judging panel to the success of the talent show format. For one thing, the judges are the constant face of the programme. Contestants come and go – week after week and series after series – so it is down to the judges to give the show its identity.

Equally important, the dynamic of the judging panel breathes life into the talent show format. Without strong personalities the show won't work. That in turn means that the format itself must provide a means for the judging panels to express those personalities.

Cowell cut his TV teeth on ITV's *Pop Idol*, a show created and owned by entertainment industry manager Simon Fuller and 19 Entertainment company. Although Cowell wasn't in charge of the show, he did have considerable influence over its development. In the early stages, contestants sang and then retired to another room while the panel discussed their performances and decided whether or not to let them through to the final stage. It was reportedly on Cowell's suggestion that all comments should be put directly to the participants and that politeness should be abandoned in favour of the plain speaking that would characterize both *Pop Idol* and *American Idol*. He saw this as a means to bring reality to the situation. In real world auditions, singers and dancers would be subjected to praise and criticism face-to-face. Cowell believed that practice should be replicated on the TV show.

But with *X Factor*, Cowell – now firmly in the driving seat – added another element to the mix. In order to increase the tension between the judges – and thus satisfy the thirst of the viewing public for drama – he introduced an element of competition.

Under *X Factor* rules, those who made it through the opening stages would be broken into four categories – boys, girls, over thirties and groups – and each of these would be mentored by one of the judges. It was an inspirational move that gave each of the judges a stake in the artists they were mentoring. At a stroke, they were no longer simply presiding impartially over a process, they were part of the action. If a particular artist failed to progress to the next stage of the show, the mentor shared some of the responsibility.

Cowell is far more than a judge with an acid tongue. Aided and abetted by his producers and fellow judges, he is a choreographer. A ringmaster.

This upped the ante when it came to on-screen rivalry between the judges. In the knockout phase of the show, each judge would be required to comment on all the performers while clearly wanting his or her own act (or acts) to do well. The temptation for Cowell, Walsh or any of the other judges was to do down the acts mentored by the other panelists while extolling the virtues of their own wards. And or course, that meant more heated on-screen exchanges.

This was arguably a variation of an old management technique. While some organizations thrive on teamwork, others seek to get the most out of their staff by setting them in direct competition with their workmates. Individual performance is rewarded while failure is penalized. For instance, there are companies who sack a percentage of sales staff every year, selecting the leavers on the basis of sales figures. It doesn't make for good teamwork, but it can, in the right circumstances, drive success. In a variation on that theme, Cowell used competitive rivalry to create compelling television.

PACKAGE THE PRODUCT

But it would be wrong to suggest that *X Factor*, *Pop Idol* and the *Got Talent* franchises were entirely down to the antics of the judges. There has always been genuine interest in the contestants and Cowell has proved clever at packaging his would-be stars to maximize their appeal.

That has been achieved in part by creating back stories. The contestants who slug it out each week are given some sort of three dimensional reality. This is again particularly true on *X Factor*. As the knockout/phone-in episodes of the show progress, the public sees a succession of carefully constructed profile films telling us who the contestants are, where they come from and what they hope to achieve. We meet their friends and family. We see their hometown. We hear soundbites from the contestants themselves, explaining why they want to win. In the meantime, the gossip columns will be doing their bit. Any hint that two *X Factor* finalists have shared a kiss – or even better a bed – will be big news.

So, as the series progresses, viewers determine their favourites not just on the basis of singing ability but also on their back stories and personalities.

That early packaging forms the basis of what is to come. When a victor is announced and the record deal is awarded, the process of image building is already underway. Anyone who makes it into the knockout round is already groomed for star status, even if the majority won't make it. By the end of the show, we'll be looking at a winner who has been taught how to dress, dance, sing more effectively and deal with the press. If all goes according to plan, the crowning of the winner will coincide with the creation of a fully-fledged pop singer.

There will still be work to do, of course, but the basics are in place to launch a recording career.

STAY TRUE TO THE BUSINESS MODEL

It's the climax of any of the new crop of talent shows. Thousands of contestants are whittled down to a final few and then, over a period of weeks, a winner is selected. The audience rejoices with the victor, and feels sympathy for the runners up. In a day or two it's all forgotten. Winners of *X Factor* or *American Idol* can be more or less guaranteed a hit but not necessarily a career. So what's the point?

By juggling the elements of a TV talent show to maximize not only viewing figures but also audience involvement, Cowell has managed to build a media brand that is bigger than any of the winners.

Think of it this way. Shows like *Pop Idol*, *American Idol* and *X Factor* have produced their fair share of successful singers but all too often the lifespan is short. For every Leona Lewis there's a forgotten hit artist who quickly returned to obscurity.

But *X Factor*, the *Got Talent* franchise and the Simon Fuller produced *American Idol* just keep on going. Every year, they pull off the same trick of involving audiences in the protracted task of filtering out contestants until a winner emerges. And while the individual winners often disappear to work on the cabaret circuit or return to day jobs, the talent shows pump out hit after hit after hit.

What's more, they've made the process of finding talent profitable in itself – the advertising revenues and cash from phone votes ensure that talent shows are self-financing, even before the money from record sales is factored in.

And for those contestants who have been lucky or talented enough to forge a long career, *X Factor* in particular has proved a useful promotional tool to keep their names in the public eye. For instance, in the 2009 knockout stage, previous winners Leona Lewis and Alexandra Burke appeared as guests. A year after winning, Burke had just launched her first solo album, so the show itself was a hugely important sales platform. Not only did she perform, but the new record was also handsomely promoted in the ad breaks.

Critics would say that in giving the people exactly what they want, Cowell is overly focused on quick returns at the expense of long-term investment in artists with genuine longevity.

This was an example of *X Factor* dominating music TV in the UK. As the only music show shown in peak time, it was not only creating chart topping acts but also promoting previous winners. Cowell probably had a right to look smug. 'You've got 14 million people watching it every week, so he doesn't need to spend anything on advertising',[3] PR expert Mark Borkowski told the *Daily Telegraph*.

Whether that's good for the long-term health of the music industry as a creative force is another question. Critics would say that in giving the people exactly what they want, Cowell is overly focused on quick returns at the expense of long-term investment in artists with genuine longevity. Yes, artists of quality have emerged from the *X Factor/American Idol/Got Talent* axis but no one would pretend that Syco has built a back catalogue of records with the potential to go on selling.

It's an unfair comparison, perhaps, but the world's big record labels do very nicely out of acts that were signed, nurtured and developed along conventional A&R lines. From the radical departures of the

Beatles and Dylan through to more modern icons in the mould of Michael Jackson and Madonna, artists that are allowed to grow and take control of their own musical direction often deliver bigger returns than purely 'manufactured' stars with a limited shelf life. They also gather core audiences that stick with them over decades.

The difference between a winner on *X Factor* and, say, a Madonna or Lady Gaga is that the latter pair (and their production handlers) are prepared to lead the audience rather than simply being led by public vote. That willingness to lead generates audience loyalty as the record buyer learns to trust the judgment of the act. That in turn lends itself to longevity. From the record point of view, that means ongoing healthy sales, plus a regular income from the back catalogue as new record buyers 'discover' an established artist.

X Factor is unlikely to uncover the next Beatles or even someone with the combination of mainstream appeal and individual artistry as with Madonna or Michael Jackson, but that probably isn't the point. Cowell's business model works for him because although the artists come and go, the show sustains itself and will go on throwing up hit artists for the foreseeable future. In doing so, it's not preventing the discovery of other types of artist, it is simply making Simon Cowell more money.

STAY IN CONTROL

And it works because he has the business side of the operation sewn up. Going back to his early TV experience on *Pop Idol*, Cowell didn't own the rights to the show – they belonged to Simon Fuller – but he did have a valuable stake in the proceedings in that his record label would be given first refusal on winners and other contestants.

Spurred by the success of *Pop Idol*, Cowell set up his production company Syco – later sold to Sony BMG. Divided into three units – music, film and TV – it has provided Cowell with a platform from which to develop a range of talent shows and other formats.

And the key to the Syco model is that it enables Cowell to exercise control over the production of multi-media projects. For instance, not only does Syco own the rights to shows such as *X Factor* and *Britain's Got Talent*, he also has first bite of the cherry signing up participants to record deals.

It's a worldwide model. The *Got Talent* format is now broadcast around the world, and in every territory Cowell earns revenue from the TV show and any associated record sales.

Which takes us back to that original question. To some extent Cowell may have handed television viewers the job of selecting talent, but he's taken care to manage that process closely through carefully constructed TV programming. And once the selection has been made and the winners announced, he has emerged as a master of exploiting their commercial potential.

HARNESS THE POWER OF THE CROWD

Through his stable of TV talent shows Cowell has pulled off the trick of letting the public select the stars of the future by means of a knockout-style competition in which viewers vote for their favourites via phone. The system not only crowns a winner by popular vote, it has also ensures that when a record is released it will sell well, not least because many of those who voted for the artist will buy his or her CDs or downloads.

X Factor alone has played a significant role in boosting UK record sales, particularly around the Christmas period, and Cowell's Syco along with partner Sony BMG are the beneficiaries.

Cowell is sourcing the wisdom of the crowd to spot winners, but it's a process that needs careful management.

- **Make the public work for you.** Cowell's use of the audience to find the stars of the future echoes a wider trend towards 'crowdsourcing' or harnessing the wisdom of the masses. Put simply, crowdsourcing means using people outside an organization to carry out work that is normally carried out internally. Many companies use crowdsourcing as a form of interactive market research. By getting members of the public to work to perform certain tasks, you can learn a lot about what your audience wants.

- **Incentivize the audience.** Cowell uses the TV audience to help him find bankable stars via phone votes. This is a form of crowdsourcing that will only work if the viewers are prepared to co-operate. To ensure their support, he works hard to create compelling television that will encourage interactivity. Whatever the crowdsource model, you have to understand the reasons why individuals may want to take part and provide appropriate incentives.

- **Act as ringmaster.** Cowell manages his shows proactively. In Britain and abroad he chooses judges that will be plain spoken and prepared to be direct with contestants and argue with each other. His judging panels often fall out and their rifts are reported in lurid detail by the tabloid press. This soap-style drama boosts ratings and engagement with the shows. The success of his shows is dependent on his willingness to lead from the front.

- **Keep the formula fresh.** Throughout his career in television, Cowell has honed the talent show formula to ensure that his shows remain fresh and compelling. When he left the UK version of *Pop Idol* to develop *X Factor* he added new features, such as a 'boot camp', and competition among judges. The shows have been kept fresh by changes to the judging panel and presentation team. Such changes have helped to keep the all-important audience watching the shows and interacting through the voting system.

- **Package the product.** Once the knockout finals begin, the contestants are carefully packaged. They are profiled on TV and the viewers find out about their lives. They become characters. When the winner emerges, he or she is already packaged as a pop star, making it easier to market the records. Again, the close involvement of the consumers informs the packaging.

- **Stay true to the business model.** When many of the singers are forgotten, *X Factor* and *Britain's Got Talent* will still be discovering new artists. Cowell has been criticized for focusing on short-term goals – the next hit – rather than developing artists in the conventional way. However, he has demonstrated that his business model works and it shows every sign of being sustainable. Like a great many successful businessmen, he is sticking to the model that works best.

- **Stay in control.** Syco has first refusal on all who take part in the shows. This means Cowell can cash in on the work done by the general public on his behalf. Getting the contractual side right has been a key factor in Cowell's financial success.

4

THINK BIG, THINK LATERAL

'Simon Cowell's genius was in colliding the music, television and telecoms businesses around a killer format. But don't forget he didn't originate that format, he just perfected it.'[1]

– Simon Walker at Maidthorn Partners, media consultancy

When rival music industry executives consider the unstoppable rise of Simon Cowell from obscure A&R man to TV and music industry mogul, they could be forgiven for asking themselves a simple question: 'Why didn't I think of that first?'

The truth of the matter is that Cowell's latter-day business model – using TV talent shows to source artists who are then signed to his record label – is both elegantly simply and bordering on pure genius.

All recording artists have to start somewhere. Sometimes they make their name as a live act before signing to a record label. Sometimes they are signed on the strength of a particularly impressive demo (demonstration) CD sent to the record label in the hope of catching the ear of someone influential. But regardless of their route in, when they get as far as recording a debut record they have a mountain to climb. A band with a loyal following of two or three hundred people – enough to pack out local gigs – suddenly has to think in terms of addressing an audience numbering hundreds of thousands. The unknown signed on a demo CD has to build an audience from scratch.

Marketing unknown acts and turning them into big stars is what record companies do. It's a hit and miss business. For every top-selling artist selling hundreds of thousands of CDs and downloads, there are dozens who will never shift enough units to cover the record label's upfront investment. So, in that regard, the record industry is a high-risk game. Rather like a venture capitalist attempting to pick the world-beating companies of the future, the failure-to-success ratio is high. Profits are made from the relatively few artists who capture the collective imagination of the target market.

Cowell's 'simple' stroke of genius has been to de-risk the process. As we've seen in previous chapters, his TV talent contests discover and effectively create popular artists long before they even set foot in a studio and sing into a microphone. The winner of *X Factor* is pretty much guaranteed a hit, if not a long-term career. And by keeping the winners coming, Cowell cashes in. Simple.

But in reality it's not so simple. *X Factor*, *Britain's Got Talent* and their brother and sister programmes around the world are complex entities, involving two media platforms – TV and the record industry – while being supported by the internet, radio, press and sponsorship deals.

The upshot is that behind a relatively simple concept, a huge amount of hard work and cross-media coordination is required. Cowell has not only thought laterally in fully exploiting the power of TV, he has thought big, and bigger.

GET THE STRUCTURE RIGHT

You can tell a lot about the intentions of a business from the way it is structured. A company that buys in products to resell to a mass audience will, most likely, be dominated by its marketing and sales departments. Technology companies have marketing and sales departments too, but they may be small when compared to the research and development function. An export-led company may well set up units to address the needs of specific overseas territories.

Since 2004, Syco has been Simon Cowell's primary commercial vehicle and, from day one, its structure has provided a large and obvious pointer to its creator's intentions.

Syco is subdivided into three business units, namely Syco Music, Syco TV and Syco Film. This three-industry structure marked a step forward in Cowell's thinking. Prior to the establishment of the new company, Cowell ran S Records. Operating as a unit of Sony BMG it was – as the name suggests – focused on music production. Cowell was using *Pop Idol* and *American Idol* to feed BMG's appetite for bankable recording artists but the rights to those shows were owned by Simon Fuller's 19 Entertainment. It was a straightforward split. Fuller's organization looked after the TV side – albeit with a huge amount of input from Cowell – while S Records recorded the winning artists and released their CDs.

Cowell was remaking himself as a multi-platform media mogul rather than simply a record label boss

So the structure of Syco indicated that Cowell was remaking himself as a multi-platform media mogul rather than simply a record label boss. The formation of the company coincided with the arrival of *X Factor*, a show devised and owned by Syco. With its TV, film and music units, Cowell's aim was to control the means of production from television show through to record release. As manager of Syco, he would be the man in charge.

Syco's music is today dominated – although not totally populated – by winners of TV talent shows. Glance at the company's portfolio and you'll find boy band Westlife (signed to S Records by Cowell in the 1990s) – and crossover opera stars Il Divo, but most of the acts currently on the label have been sourced via *X Factor* or *Britain's Got Talent*. Shayne Ward, the first *X Factor* winner is there, as are Alexandra Burke, Susan Boyle and US breakthrough artist Leona Lewis. All of the label's artists have had hit records, a boast that few other record companies or production houses can match.

Syco Music's 100% record as a hitmaker can be attributed to its sister unit. Syco TV was set up to produce entertainment-themed reality TV shows. If it wasn't for these shows – *X Factor* being the flagship – the recorded music side of the business wouldn't be nearly as successful.

X Factor is one of the most popular shows on British television and – for good or ill – it is the only prime-time music show running regularly on any of the major networks. Once upon a time, the BBC's *Top of the Pops* provided the main route to the television audience for mainstream pop acts. With that show long gone, *X Factor* has come to define what British pop music is and how it is presented. And while *Top of the Pops* reflected the whole gamut of popular music, from rap and rock to novelty songs, *X Factor* is about Cowell's vision. He owns the show, owns the successful acts and, if and when he signs them to his label, dictates the course of their careers.

The same is true, to some extent, of Syco TV's second big commission for the UK market – *Britain's Got Talent*. As a more generalist talent show it doesn't necessarily throw up singers or potential recording artists as winners, but has nonetheless proved successful in finding artists for the Syco label. These include opera singer Paul Potts, winner of the first show, and Susan Boyle.

That relationship between Syco Music and Syco TV is there on the screen for all to see but the television production unit is also swelling the coffers of Cowell and joint-venture partner Sony by successfully marketing and selling programmes and programme formats around the world.

We'll be looking at this in greater detail in a later chapter but for now it's worth saying that both the *X Factor* and *Got Talent* concepts have found a global audience. While drama and comedy originated in the UK doesn't necessarily travel well abroad, the brand of reality TV purveyed by Syco appears to have a near universal appeal. Perhaps that's not surprising. Every culture has an entertainment industry and wherever you go in the world there is never a shortage of people who not only long to perform but also see a singing or dancing career as the way to break out of a humdrum life. Syco TV's productions tap into the desire to lead a life less ordinary. And for those who don't perform, the human drama of the knockout phases of Syco shows has also proved universally compelling.

The establishment of Syco TV has provided Cowell with a third benefit. Success on *Pop Idol* has brought him to the attention of TV executives around the world and his ability to fashion compelling shows is widely respected. With a small production team in place, he is in a strong position to develop and sell new concepts. This won't always deliver success on the scale of *X Factor*. For instance, in the US, *American Inventor* – a show produced in partnership with entrepreneur Peter Jones – won the all-important second series but didn't make it to a third. Meanwhile in the UK, a show designed to find the cast for a new production of *Grease the Musical*, is generally agreed to have underperformed.

Nevertheless, Syco TV provides the means for Cowell to rejuvenate his portfolio of shows. The chances are that at some time in the future the current crop of Cowell shows will slip down the ratings. His plan must surely be to have replacements waiting in the wings.

The film unit has been less active to date, although there are a number of projects in the pipeline, including *Star Struck*, said to be a *Fame*-style picture, themed around a talent show.

HIRE THE RIGHT PEOPLE

It's tempting to think of Cowell as a one-man band. A force of nature carrying all before him. A lord of all he surveys. A puppet master pulling the strings while maintaining tight control of his ever-expanding Syco empire. That would be misleading. He is certainly the boss, but gathered around him is a strong team of experienced people from the television and music industries.

That shouldn't be a surprise. Even the relatively simple process of making and marketing a record is all about teamwork and harnessing the skills of a diverse group of people.

Behind the singer or band, there are the backroom men and women who write the songs, play the instruments, programme the computers and engineer the sounds. Then there are the marketing experts who take the singer and song and present them to the world. They in turn are backed up by photographers, stylists, make-up artists and copy writers. It's a team game.

> **It's tempting to think of Cowell as a one-man band. That would be misleading. He is certainly the boss, but gathered around him is a strong team of experienced people.**

Making television programmes is, if anything, more complex; and when you bring the two media platforms together through programmes such as *X Factor*, you're looking at coordinating the activities of a small army of industry professionals and front-of-house talent.

Cowell himself is a music industry veteran who in the latter part of his career has demonstrated the same instincts for creating compelling TV as he did for nurturing pop talent. But he certainly didn't make *X Factor* happen alone. A glance at the Syco TV team sheet shows that Cowell is working with some of the most experienced people in the business.

For instance, in 2006, Simon Jones assumed the role of Vice President with responsibility for selling Syco's programmes internationally while developing ancillary businesses for the company's artists and formats.

Jones and Cowell have a shared history. As managing director of TV production company Fremantle, Jones played an important part in getting *Pop Idol* onto British screens, pitching the concept to the US and selling the format internationally. He also worked closely with Cowell on the launch of *X Factor*.

The shows are about creating moments that will be talked about through the week. They start a national conversation.

Syco TV's director of programmes, Nigel Hall, is another industry heavyweight. Having climbed his way up the TV production ladder, he produced hit shows such as *Stars in their Eyes* and *You've been Framed* for UK TV and, prior to joining Syco in 2003, he achieved the heady position of Programme Controller at Granada Television.

An admirer of Cowell's work on *Pop Idol*, he attempted to sign the up-and-coming TV personality and mogul to host a quiz show. Instead, Cowell offered him a job.

Like Cowell, Hall knows his respective businesses from the bottom up. Leaving school in Stockport with just one O level he headed down to London with the intention of working in TV. After a spell of employment in a shoe shop, he managed to wedge a foot in the industry door when he secured a job as a copy taker for BBC News. From there he moved to a lowly floor manager's position at ITV and began a climb through the industry hierarchy to director and producer positions.

Meanwhile over at Syco Music, Cowell has taken care to put similarly talented people in key positions. A case in point is David Gray, hired in 2009 as Senior Vice President of A&R.

Gray has an impressive industry track record, including hands-on experience of making records as a songwriter and recording artist in his own right. As an A&R man and record company executive he has worked with a range of artists, including Duran Duran, the Jonas Brothers and Cyndi Lauper. Significantly, Gray was appointed when based in the US. He will continue to operate out of New York, with a remit to build Syco's presence in the US at a time when the launch of *X Factor* in the American market is expected to generate new opportunities for the company.

In a similar move, Syco announced in March 2010 that it was hiring Ellis Watson to oversee the expansion of the company's operations in the US. Watson clearly had the credentials for the job. As managing director of Celador International, he oversaw one of the most impressive overseas sales operations in the history of British television when he rolled out the format for *Who Wants to be a Millionaire?*

After Celador, he stepped back from the entertainment business for a while to work for transport company Firstgroup, but Cowell's offer lured him back. 'I've got the most exciting job in entertainment anywhere in the world – it's not a vocation, it's a calling', he said in a statement.

Cowell is often regarded as the public face of Syco, but managing director Sonny Takhar – who also happens to be a share-owning partner in the company – also plays a front-line role. Although he remains very much in Cowell's shadow, Takhar is often the public face of Syco when a business announcement is to be made. When an artist is signed or another record goes to number one, the chances are it is he who will speak to the press.

And, perhaps surprisingly, Takhar is frequently the man that reporters turn to for clues to the record label's strategic direction or its approach to promoting an artist. For instance, when it was decided that Leona Lewis should return to *X Factor* – to promote her latest album rather than compete – it was Takhar who fielded the questions. Lewis had by then emerged as a world-class act, so questions were asked as to whether an appearance on a reality show would undermine her status. At first glance, this would seem a natural issue for the outspoken Cowell to deal with but it was former RCA executive Takhar who said, 'We'd be mad not to. *The X Factor* is the biggest show on TV right now – it makes total sense.'

Indeed, the strategy outlined by Takhar neatly illustrated Syco's 'think big, think lateral' philosophy. By returning to the show that made her, Lewis was shining some of her own recently acquired star quality on the latest crop of competitors and promoting herself to a television audience of around 13 to 14 million at the same time. In the world of Syco, every angle is covered.

The fact that Cowell surrounds himself with people who are well respected within the industry is nothing less than good practice. As organizations grow they become more complex and, if the founder attempts to maintain tight control of every aspect of the operation, the likelihood is that everything will grind to a halt as

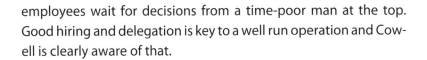

employees wait for decisions from a time-poor man at the top. Good hiring and delegation is key to a well run operation and Cowell is clearly aware of that.

BRING PARTNERS ON BOARD

In addition to his in-house team – which also includes music creative director Tim Byrne and TV development head Siobhan Greene – Cowell has also established strong working links with the wider television industry.

The key partnership is with Fremantle, a global television conglomerate that can trace its history back to 1917. Owned by the RTL Group – itself 90% owned by German media giant Bertelsmann – Fremantle produces and creates television programmes and concepts for the global marketplace. And it has to be said, it's been hugely successful both as a creator and a distributor.

As a production company, Fremantle has a hand in just about every programme genre, ranging from drama (*The Bill*, *Neighbours*, *Baywatch*), to comedy (*Mr Bean*) and children's programming (*Button Moon*, *Rainbow*, *Wind in the Willows*). Thanks to the success of *X Factor* and the *Pop Idol* franchise it is perhaps best known as a producer of reality TV and one of its key money spinners is selling on the programme formats that have been successful in one country to television executives elsewhere in the world.

Given Cowell's global ambitions, Fremantle is, in many ways, the ideal bedfellow. As things stand at the moment, the company has production facilities in 22 countries around the world and it sells its shows in more than 150 countries. In other words, it has the infrastructure in place to actively sell programmes off-the-peg and license formats, while also possessing the skills, hardware and studio space to make programmes for its international customers.

It doesn't stop there. Fremantle distribution business extends to DVDs for the home entertainment market and increasingly the company is licensing brands for use on other platforms such as video games.

Nestling within Fremantle's group structure is the UK production company Talkback Thames, the entity that provides the wherewithal to bring *X Factor* and *Britain's Got Talent* to UK screens.

The relationship between Talkback and Syco has been mutually beneficial. Syco gains from the programme-making expertise of a production company formed through a merger of Thames Television – once a broadcaster forming part of the ITV Network – and successful production company Talkback.

Meanwhile, Talkback Thames has seen its profits rise sharply thanks to its association with Cowell and is portfolio of shows. Chief executive Lorraine Heggessey acknowledged the importance of the relationship when she spoke to the *Daily Telegraph* in 2010. Fielding questions over concern that the roll out of *X Factor* in the US would ultimately mean an end to the Syco/Thames Talkback relationship, she was quick to quash that strand of speculation while also signalling the company's determination to maintain the link: 'We are Simon's production partner, we have worked with him for many years and we have a team he respects … I'm not going to lose him.'[2]

Heggessey's comments underline the importance of partnerships, not just for Cowell and his extended family of collaborators. In business, partnerships exist to help the parties involved deliver on a commercial goal and if the association works well the best advice is often to stick with it.

USE ALL MEDIA OUTLETS

While Cowell's business model is based on a symbiotic relationship between the music and television industries, the success of *X Factor* and *Britain's Got Talent*, along with similar shows overseas, has been enhanced by clever use of complementary media platforms.

Syco TV shows don't exist in the vacuum of Saturday night programme schedules. Viewers don't simply switch on at 8pm and tune out at 9pm. The shows create moments that will be talked about through the week. They start a national conversation.

The press plays an important role in keeping the bandwagon rolling in the dead time between one weekend and the next. The contestants are profiled, any hint of a scandal or love tryst will make it onto the tabloid front pages and columnists have their say on who was hot and who was not.

TV plays a similar role. A contestant voted out on Saturday or Sunday will inevitably spend the following week doing the rounds of breakfast TV and light entertainment chat shows. There will be plenty of tea and sympathy and a few more minutes of fame that will last at least until the next participant is voted out.

But arguably the real 'national conversation' takes place elsewhere – not least on the internet. Reality TV and the internet fit together hand in glove. On social networks and blogs the events we see on-screen have what Heggessey calls 'the talk-about ability fac-tor'[3]. They are discussed, dissected and argued over by the public at large. There are Facebook groups dedicated to the shows them-selves and the contestants. Some are official, others put together by fans and/or critics.

The internet footprints of *X Factor* and *Britain's Got Talent* undoubt-edly boost ratings and, thus, the ability of the show to secure top dollar from advertisers. Equally important, the shows' official web-sites generate revenue in their own right, with companies inter-ested in investing or sponsorship, like Talk Talk and Xbox.

Add to that the revenue from the phone votes and calls to shows such as *The Xtra Factor* and you have a nice little earner in terms of incremental revenues, with the cash being split between the production companies and ITV.

Cowell sees the internet (as accessed via PCs and mobiles) as an increasingly important delivery channel for shows and music. As far back as 2006, he told the *Telegraph*: '… once mobile phones are able to carry this stuff much easier, you've suddenly got billions of consumers who want to see your content.'[4]

Since then the success of the Apple iPhone has revolutionized the mobile market. With a big touch screen and rental deals via mobile companies that usually offer the consumer unlimited access to the internet via fast 3G networks, the device has created genuine demand for web content and streamed video accessible on the move. Pro-grammes such as *X Factor* have been natural beneficiaries.

And if *X Factor* and *Got Talent* represent the ultimate in reality TV/game-show crossover why not take the formula and transfer it to a video game?

Why not indeed? Plans are currently in the offing to release versions of *X Factor* for Xbox, PS3 and PC platforms. Created by Deep Silver and Fremantle Media and announced in June 2010, the game is to be distributed in countries that run the series on their national TV networks.

Cowell was quick to realize the commercial potential of a mutually beneficial relationship between TV and the music industry.

It would be surprising if Cowell and his partners failed to exploit the potential to engage consumers through interactive media. After all Cowell was quick to realize the commercial potential of a mutually beneficial relationship between TV and the music industry. The internet, mobile phone and video games markets represent a natural extension of that all-embracing, lateral thinking strategy.

THINK BIG, THINK LATERAL

Simon Cowell's basic idea – create a TV show, discover talent and sell that talent back to viewers via music CDs and downloads – is elegantly simple but making it work requires attention to organization and partnerships with companies that have the wherewithal to deliver content across multiple platforms.

- **Get the structure right.** Cowell's Syco – a joint venture with Sony – is subdivided into music, TV and film divisions. Although employing relatively few people, its specialist units mean that Syco is able to coordinate its TV and record production activities. In all business ventures it is vital to get the structure of the business right.

- **Hire the right people.** Cowell isn't a one man band. At Syco he's working alongside a team of people with wide ranging experience in the television and music industries. Rather than attempt to be a jack of all trades and master of none, he has hired senior people who really know their respective industries. This is good management practice. Businesses that are overly reliant on one man or woman may operate efficiently for a period of time but few leaders will have the time or the skills to manage all the functions of a complex organization. It is better to delegate to people you trust.
- **Bring partners on board.** Syco is a small operation and, on its own, it wouldn't be in a position to bring programmes such as *X Factor* and *Got Talent* to the screen. In the UK, Syco works with Talkback Thames, a production company with a long and impressive track record. Talkback is a subsidiary of global media company Fremantle. Fremantle's international presence has enabled Cowell to market his TV concepts around the world. The partnerships work because each partner brings its own skills and resources to the table. For Cowell, long-standing partnerships have provided his small operation with the technical and creative support it needs to deliver on its commercial goals.
- **Use all media outlets.** *X Factor* and *Got Talent* generate a national conversation. Those who watch the shows want to share their view and know more about the contestants and the judges. Social media and blogging sites – notably Facebook and Twitter – play an important part in keeping interest in the shows alive from week to week. Cowell is keen to strike deals to provide content to mobile operators. His strategy reflects a much wider trend that has seen businesses embracing new digital channels to market their products.

5

DEVELOP INTERNATIONAL FORMATS

'The trick for production companies such as Fremantle … is to turn programmes into entertainment brands.'[1]

– Gerhard Zeiler, Fremantle

Pick up a newspaper profile of Simon Cowell and the chances are you'll find a considerable number of column inches dedicated to his popularity on both sides of the Atlantic. As famous in the US for judging *American Idol* as he is in the UK for his performances on *X Factor*, Cowell spends much of his time commuting between homes in London and Los Angeles where he lives amid the mansions of Beverley Hills.

All this is ideal fare for the tabloid newspapers. Cowell is the Brit who has cracked the US in a big, big way. *American Idol* is America's top-rated show, and as with *X Factor* in the UK, Cowell is undoubtedly the star. Just as newspapers in the UK follow each twist and turn of Cowell's on- and off-screen relationships with fellow judges such as Louis Walsh and Cheryl Cole, the American press provides similar blow-by-blow commentary on spats with the *American Idol* panellists.

Cowell's profile in the US can't be underestimated. *Idol* is a key show for the Fox Network. Not only is it the company's biggest success in terms of ratings, it is also a crucial factor in delivering audiences for its other shows. For instance, the viewing figures for shows such as *House* and *24* have been boosted by a position in the schedules next to Cowell and company.

Cowell himself clearly loves the American lifestyle and, perhaps more importantly, the US attitude to success. 'Look, I was slightly cynical of the American mentality before I came over here,' he told the *New York Times* in 2004, 'but now I preach it. Here, no one's going to tear you down if you buy yourself a $300,000 car. They're likely to say: "Well, you probably worked hard for it. Good luck to you."'[2]

But in 2010, Cowell announced that he was to part company with *American Idol*, a show in which he was, when all was said and done, an employee. Instead, he would focus his energies on bringing the Syco-owned *X Factor* to US screens while also developing new concepts for the international television market.

This was big and potentially bad news for the Fox Network. Commenting on Cowell's decision to quit *American Idol*, the company did its best to play down the significance of the move, saying in a statement that '*Idol* was bigger than any one person'.

Not everyone agreed. Talking to the *New York Times* on the day Cowell announced his decision to quit, veteran TV executive Fred Silverman predicted that the star's departure would take much of the polish off the *American Idol* silver. 'He's the voice everybody wants to hear,' Mr. Silverman said. 'It doesn't mean the show will fail without him. But it will be nowhere near as successful as it was in its heyday.'[3]

Cowell's decision to quit *American Idol* came as a surprise to no one. The show has made him a star in the US, certainly – earning him around £20m a year in the process – but Cowell is, first and foremost, a businessman. Outside the *Idol* studio, Syco's shows were having huge success around the world and Cowell was understandably keen to roll out his company's most successful concept – *X Factor* – in the world's biggest and most lucrative television marketplace.

And these days, selling the formats of successful Syco-owned shows is key to Cowell's business strategy. As things stand, you can see versions of *X Factor* in 40 countries around the world while shows based on the *Got Talent* format are shown in more than 30 territories. By selling formats, Cowell has become an international television industry player.

This is great news for the Cowell bank balance. Overseas television companies pay for the shows and when the viewers have had their day and a winner is crowned, Syco has first option on releasing a record. And while Cowell continues to appear on judging panels in the UK and US, in the vast majority of territories, the sheer hard work of producing a programme, getting it onto the air and attracting an audience is done by TV companies working locally. It's an arrangement that means Cowell's empire of overseas sales can grow rapidly without stretching the resources of Syco too thinly around the world.

SEIZE THE MARKET OPPORTUNITIES

An ambitious television producer with a hit show on his hands and an eye for international sales has two choices – either attempt to sell the show as a completed product to foreign broadcasters or sell the format itself.

Selling a show can be difficult if it is constructed in the UK for a UK audience – it won't necessarily travel well. For instance, a comedy starring British actors, spiced with jokes that the home audience will understand probably won't be right for an overseas audience. The same principle applies to drama.

That's not to say it can't be done. The BBC's *Doctor Who* sells around the world, while the very Australian *Neighbours* has long been a feature of teatime viewing in the UK. But it is difficult. Take critically acclaimed US dramas such as *The Wire*, *Madmen* and *The Sopranos*. They are shown in the UK but usually late at night on minority stations. Despite the applause of critics, they can't compete with home-grown products in terms of ratings.

The alternative is to sell the format. For instance, Ricky Gervais enjoyed a certain amount of success in the US market with his situation comedy, *The Office*. But it wasn't until he sold the format of the show – thus allowing it to be remade with American actors – that it really took off with an audience that extended beyond the comedy cognoscenti.

Over the last few years, British production companies have been enjoying something of a boom in the sale of formats to overseas markets. Indeed, in 2009, Britain's share of the format sales market jumped from an already healthy 29% to a world leading 41%.

The focus tends to be on game shows and reality TV. There's a good reason for this. Even if you change the cast and introduce scripts tailored for the target audience, it can be hard to get a drama or a comedy to work outside its home area. So while Ricky Gervais succeeded royally in adapting *The Office* for US viewers, a licensed remake of the hit British drama series *Life on Mars* failed in the American market, as did a version of the hit drama *Prime Suspect*. Arguably, the majority of comedies and dramas simply carry too much cultural baggage that relates directly to their country or origin. You can change the actors, the language and (very often) the scripts, but even if everything is localized, the underlying concept often doesn't work.

Commenting on Cowell's decision to quit *American Idol*, the company did its best to play down the significance of the move, saying in a statement that 'Idol was bigger than any one person'.

Game and reality shows have proved to be a much easier sell. Over the last few years we've seen Britain's commercial and public service broadcasters lay out their stalls at television festivals around the world and ring up healthy sales.

For instance, the BBC has scored major successes with *The Weakest Link* (shown in 60 countries), *Strictly Come Dancing* (30 countries) and *The Office*. Meanwhile ITV's *Who Wants to be a Millionaire?* – produced by Celador and owned by Sony Television – has been broadcast in around 100 territories. The worldwide popularity and profile of the 'Millionaire' franchise is such that a low budget film, *Slumdog Millionaire*, plotted around India's version of the show, won eight Oscars and achieved worldwide success.

An ambitious television producer with a hit show on his hands has two choices – either attempt to sell the show as a completed product or sell the format itself.

The success of *Slumdog Millionaire* illustrates how formats work internationally. When a game or reality TV show is sold to an overseas broadcaster, some elements of the original programme will be jettisoned or adapted to suit the tastes of the local audience, but the overall look and feel is usually retained.

That was good news for the maker's of *Slumdog Millionaire*. A cinema goer in Wisconsin who knew the US version of the programme would instantly recognize the Indian show as depicted in the film. From the style of the scoreboard through to well-known features such as 'phone-a-friend', it was a familiar landscape. Thus, just as the programme itself had travelled around the world, a drama based on the programme could also travel.

Strong formats are in demand for a number of reasons. First and foremost, if a game or reality show has been successful in one country, there is a strong possibility that it will succeed elsewhere in the world as well. And as the broadcaster or production company in the home market has already done the research and development, a licensed show is relatively cheap to launch.

For producers it can mean a big pay cheque. A show that airs in 30 countries around the world generates multiple revenue streams. What's more, the companies who buy in the format do – or at least pay for – most of the work. They hire the stars, they build the sets, sell commercials, secure the sponsorship deals and market the shows to their domestic audience. Thus the global market for successful formats represents a huge opportunity to rights owners who can sit back and watch the royalty payments roll in. It's an opportunity that Cowell has been eager to exploit through worldwide sales of *Got Talent* and *X Factor*.

EXPLOIT YOUR PROFILE

These days *X Factor* and *Got Talent* are as recognizable internationally as *Who Wants to be a Millionaire?* or *The Weakest Link*. However, Cowell is probably unique among those who create or hold the right to the formats because he is as well known as his shows. Few of us could name the creator of *Who Wants to be a Millionaire?* or *The Weakest Link* but in the UK and US, at least, Cowell is recognized as both the star and the mastermind behind *X Factor* and *Got Talent*.

Cowell's profile in the US has been an important factor in getting a green light for shows such as *America's Got Talent*, *American Inventor* and the soon-to-be-launched *X Factor*. Ironically, his profile has been largely generated by the success of *American Idol*, a show owned originally by business partner Simon Fuller's 19 Entertainment.

But although Cowell doesn't own any rights to *American Idol*, he did play an important role in getting the US version of *Pop Idol* onto the screen. In 2001 – the same year that *Pop Idol* launched in the UK – he flew to the US with Simon Fuller and producer Simon Jones to pitch the show to TV executives. It was an ambitious move. *Pop Idol* had been a huge success in Britain and many production teams would have focused their energies on a second UK series. Even in the dawning era of format TV, the US market was notoriously difficult to crack, so it would probably have been easier for Cowell and company to rest on their laurels and bask in their UK success.

But in many ways, *Pop Idol/American Idol* could have been designed with the US market in mind. Its key elements – talent, competition, the realization of long-held ambitions – are perfectly in tune with the American dream. It's an indicator of their business savvy that Fuller and Cowell recognized the potential of the show to appeal to a US audience after just one series in the UK.

The team pitched the good old-fashioned way, by making appointments with TV executives, and it wasn't an easy ride. At least two broadcasters said no to the concept before it was finally taken on board by Fox, the network owned by Rupert Murdoch's News International. Even that success didn't initially seem like a ringing endorsement. According to Cowell's unofficial biographer Chas Newkey-Burden[4] the pitch went badly, with network executives showing little interest. But, as luck would have it, Rupert Murdoch's daughter Elisabeth was a fan of *Pop Idol* in the UK. She contacted her father and advised him that the show would be a hit. Once the matter was in the hands of the organ grinder rather than the monkeys it was pretty much a done deal. Murdoch reportedly phoned Peter Chernin, News Corporation's president and instructed him to buy. Victory had been snatched from the jaws of defeat and both Cowell and Fuller were on the road to US success.

It wasn't quite a straightforward format deal. Cowell was known to be the star of the UK version and Fox was keen to have him on board as a judge on *American Idol*. Cowell wavered, fearing the workload would be too much but ultimately he said yes. It was a decision that would change his career, allowing him to complete the journey from little-known record company executive through to major international star.

As was the case in the UK, Cowell received a double reward. Good money from the US network and – with his record company hat on – first pick of the winners.

GO GLOBAL

America has been good to Simon Cowell. In addition to his work on *American Idol* he has so far launched two shows under the Syco banner – *American Inventor* and *America's Got Talent* – and the US version of *X Factor* is on the way. But it's important to remember that the Cowell empire now extends well beyond the US. Working in partnership with Fremantle Media, Syco is expanding its global reach with the sale of its formats around the world.

The *Got Talent* franchise is a case in point. The show was originally planned to launch in the UK, hosted by comedian Paul O'Grady. Plans for the launch were temporarily shelved when O'Grady left the project. As a result the format was given its first try out on US television in 2006. It was a major hit, even without Cowell on the judging panel.

Since then the *Got Talent* franchise has spread around the world like wildfire. In the space of a few short years Cowell's take on the good old-fashioned TV talent show has taken root in Europe, Asia,

Australia and America. From Germany, France and Spain to Russia, Slovenia and Serbia, the show crosses Europe from East to West. Equally, a traveller setting out on a journey along the Pan American highway can see versions of the show from Argentina up to Canada. It's even enlivening the airwaves of the Pacific region, from the Philippines to Australia and New Zealand.

***Pop Idol/American Idol* could have been designed with the US market in mind. Its key elements are perfectly in tune with the American dream**

It's a similar story with *X Factor*. Due to Cowell's contractual relationship with *American Idol*'s producers, its arrival in the US has been delayed but elsewhere in the world, versions of the show are hugely popular.

Selling these shows hasn't been a particularly hard slog. The global TV market has been expanding rapidly and broadcasters are hungry for successful shows. Speaking to the *Financial Times* in 2007, Gerhard Zeiler, chief executive of Fremantle Media's parent company RTL, described how the international media landscape has changed from a time when programmes had to do well for several months to a year before even considering taking it overseas: 'Now if something is a hit in the UK or the US you can bet you'll achieve a worldwide roll-out in at least 10 countries within a year.'[5] As they compete for audiences distracted by numerous new media alternatives, large broadcasters have had to build global research departments to scour other markets for ideas, he says.

The key, of course, is to have a successful show and that's where Cowell's track record of success in the UK and US has been vital. In the case of the American version, TV executives the world over could see a show that had risen to the top of ratings in the world's toughest and most competitive television market.

The UK version of *Got Talent* has been an equally successful shop window, not only in terms of its UK audience figures but also the international interest in the acts it discovers. For instance, when Scottish singer Susan Boyle wowed UK viewers with her version of 'I dreamed a dream' her fame didn't begin and end within the borders of the UK. The clip of her debut performance was made available on YouTube where millions of other people watched her performance. It was the surprise factor that generated the hits. Boyle was an ordinary middle-aged woman, lacking in glamour and, some would argue, social skills. Little was expected of her when she walked on to the stage of *Britain's Got Talent* and the quality and power of her singing voice caught everyone off guard. The applause at the end of her performance was genuine and heartfelt. A star had been created. It was a water cooler moment for British TV, transformed into an international media event by the power of the internet.

Boyle's barnstorming appearance on *Britain's Got Talent* probably guaranteed her some kind of record deal and although she didn't win, she was signed by Cowell. Equally important for the Cowell bank balance, the fact that she became a global talking point raised the profile of the show even further, enhancing the sales potential of the format.

THINK LOCAL WHEN YOU ACT GLOBAL

Selling a television format to an overseas market is something of a balancing act. On the one hand, you want to retain all the elements of the show that have made it popular in its home market. Equally, though, it's important to tweak the format to suit the local audience.

When *Pop Idol* first appeared on US television, the concept mirrored that of the UK version. The presence of Cowell as 'Mr Nasty' provided continuity – arguably ensuring that *American Idol* retained the main selling point of its UK counterpart – and care was taken to find other judges who offered an effective counterbalance. US record industry stalwart Randy Jackson and singer Paula Abdul were brought on board, providing a warmer foil to Cowell's acerbic Brit. On the presenter front, the UK version had Newcastle comedians Ant and Dec playing a double-headed compère role and this was echoed by the decision to hire comic Brian Dunkleman and DJ Ryan Seacrest to host the US version. The mechanics of choosing a pop idol – from open auditions to knockout phase – were also pretty much identical.

But local versions of international hit shows don't have to be slavish in their adherence to the original format, and Syco's shows are often adapted significantly before hitting the airwaves of markets outside the UK.

For instance, any comparison of local versions of the *Got Talent* franchise reveals a whole range of differences, driven by the culture of the market in question and the budgets available to broadcasters.

Prize money is a case in point. In the US, winners receive a $1m prize; in Germany it is 100,000 Euro while in Belgium winners can expect to receive a mere 50,000 Euro. The titles reflect national sensibilities too. In egalitarian China, the show's title translates as *Everyone's Got Talent*, while other variations on the theme include *Super Talent* and *What's Your Talent?*

The competition format doesn't usually vary to a great degree from the original model but even then there are exceptions. In China, the weekly shows feature different acts rather than the more usual format of thousands of people being filtered down to just one winner through open auditions and a knockout stage.

SELL THE ORIGINAL PRODUCT

It's not always formats that sell – it's also possible to sell a show tailored for one market into another. For instance, when *X Factor* launches on US TV on the Fox Network, the same show will also be aired in Canada via CTV. So why not make a local version of the show specifically for Canada? The short answer is, a Canadian version would not feature Simon Cowell. In showing the US version, Canadian TV gets the main ratings driver. 'Simon Cowell is *The X Factor*,' said Susanne Boyce, president of creative and content at CTV, 'He's a No.1 brand and a natural fit for our network. *The X Factor* is one of the most successful series in the world right now and we're excited to bring it to Canadians on CTV.'[6]

Meanwhile, UK viewers who can't get enough of Cowell concepts can watch the bought-in *America's Got Talent* on ITV while looking forward to the British counterpart later in the year. In other words, the makers are selling not one but two versions of the same programme into the domestic schedules.

It's a good trick. In many ways selling the format of a television show is like a manufacturing business licensing its intellectual property to allow a partner to make a particular product in an overseas territory. The owner of the intellectual property receives royalties on the overseas sales while the manufacturing partner does the bulk of the work in terms of production and marketing. Usually the contractual agreements surrounding these agreements prevent the owner of the IP from selling its own products into the partner's market.

But with television it's different. A company like Syco can license local versions of the show while also – in some territories at least – selling the British or American originals into the same territory. This is possible because the two products complement each other rather than compete. Fans of *Britain's Got Talent* on the main ITV channel will also watch *America's Got Talent* on ITV's supplementary digital channels. The ratings achieved by one don't undermine the viewing figures for the other. Indeed, the presence of the US show on a UK channel arguably whets the appetite for the next series of the UK version.

LOOK TO THE FUTURE

It remains to be seen whether Cowell's success in selling Syco products overseas can continue. At the moment, the signs are positive. *X Factor* is a global show and its arrival in the US can only boost its revenue earning potential. Meanwhile, Cowell has an experienced international partner in the shape of Fremantle Media, a company with huge experience selling into the international television marketplace.

If there are storm clouds ahead it's simply that trends in the television market come and go. As things stand, British TV is having a field day in terms of international format sales, but the pipeline isn't looking quite so healthy. In April 2010, the *Guardian* newspaper noted that enthusiasm for British formats was on the wane following a series of high profile failures.[7] Citing a report in industry bible *The Hollywood Reporter*, the paper revealed that for the first time in a decade UK production companies had failed to get any of their formats to the stage where they would be piloted by a US Network.

So the launch of *X Factor* in the US is not only an important step for Cowell, it could be something of a watershed for the UK television industry. Its success could drive renewed interest in British concepts. Meanwhile, Cowell has pledged to continue developing new formats for the international market. Keeping things fresh is all important.

It remains to be seen if he can maintain the momentum. The launch of *X Factor* in the US has generated a huge amount of excitement within the television and music industries and, given Cowell's popularity, it is expected to be a ratings topper for some time to come.

It's a dilemma that faces all mature businesses. Do you stick with what you know or diversify into new types of products?

But when *X Factor* and *Got Talent* ratings begin to slip there could be some real challenges ahead. If he sticks with the devil he knows – talent shows – then he will have to pull off the trick of creating something that is different enough to revive the format while retaining the successful link between the popularity of the TV show and ongoing record sales. If he branches out – and we've seen him do that already with *American Inventor* – he's sailing into unchartered waters where the rewards may not be so great.

It's a dilemma that faces all mature businesses. Do you stick with what you know or diversify into new types of products? It will be fascinating to see how Cowell's strategy evolves.

DEVELOP INTERNATIONAL FORMATS

Building on his success in both the UK and the US, Simon Cowell has successfully sold the format of *X Factor* and *Got Talent* into television markets around the world. This is how he's done it.

- **Seize the market opportunities.** Over the last few years, British companies have been hugely successful in selling 'formats' developed for the UK market to overseas buyers. These include game shows such as *Who Wants to be a Millionaire?*, reality shows, dramas and comedies. There is huge demand for shows that have proven successful in home markets. Cowell has taken advantage of this demand. Working with distribution partner Fremantle, Syco has sold *X Factor* and *Got Talent* around the world. It's a classic example of identifying demand in overseas markets and marketing the product accordingly.

- **Exploit your profile.** After the UK, Cowell's big success was in the US. His work as a judge on *American Idol* gave him a profile and standing that proved invaluable when pitching his own *American Inventor* and *Got Talent* concepts to US executives. The shows themselves also have a profile internationally. For instance, Susan Boyle's show stopping performance on *Britain's Got Talent* was watched around the world, with YouTube playing a big part in its dissemination. Global interest in the UK show can only help international sales of the format itself. It's a demonstration that success in a foreign marketplace depends not only on the quality of the product but on the track record of the company behind it.

- **Go global.** When Cowell and partner Simon Fuller tasted success with *Pop Idol* it would have been easy for them to rest on their laurels and focus on the UK market. Instead, recognizing the appeal to the US market they took the idea to American networks at a time when the British show was still settling in. Today Cowell and his partners are still very much focused on international sales and by selling the formats (the intellectual property) to local TV companies, Syco has grown its empire without stretching its own resources too thinly. Licensing product is a great way to grow internationally. Business models range from franchising and licensing a band through to licensing manufacture.

- **Think local when you act global.** When selling products into an international market, it's often necessary to tailor the packaging and the product itself to local tastes and culture. Though Syco's shows are recognizable around the world, some aspects of the branding and presentational style are different.

- **Sell the original product.** Two versions of the same product can be sold into the same market, provided the products are complementary. For instance, viewers in the UK can watch the British and US versions of *Got Talent* on the ITV network. The appetite for one feeds demand for the other.

- **Look to the future.** In business, you can't rest on your laurels. Today's successful product may be much less popular two or three years down the line. Cowell recognizes the need to keep things fresh and has pledged to develop new TV formats. Continuing R&D is vital for business success.

6

WORK WITH PARTNERS

'I know my comfort area, which is why I get it right more than I get it wrong.'[1]

– Simon Cowell

Simon Cowell has never been a one-man band. While much of his success is down to his own drive, understanding of the market and willingness to experiment, he is also a team player. Throughout his career he has worked successfully with some of the biggest names in the music industry.

Partnership has been a recurring theme in the Cowell biography. In the early days of his career he left the comfort zone of EMI records to work first with Ellis Rich on the launch of E&S Records and then with Iain Burton at Fanfare Records. Cowell played a senior role in both these young companies. He had the opportunity to learn about the industry while making his own decisions and mistakes.

Some of these partnerships have endured to this day, including Cowell's partnership with Pete Waterman. The two men worked together at Fanfare Records and went on to sit together on the judging panel for the *Pop Idol* series and they remain friends, despite a few well publicized ups and downs in their personal relationship. Cowell acknowledges that he learned a huge amount about developing and managing talent and creating hit records from a man who was part of a formidable hit-making machine – Stock Aitkin and Waterman – at a time when Cowell was just beginning to taste success. These days, Waterman's profile as a music industry mogul has been long eclipsed by that of Cowell, but it's widely accepted that he played a huge role in getting the younger man's career out of second gear and into the fast lane.

But perhaps the most important personal partnership in Cowell's recent career is his association with another high profile industry figure, Simon Fuller.

By the early 2000s Cowell was an established hit maker, with a successful portfolio of artists in his S Records/BMG stable. Top selling records by Five, Westlife and Robson and Jerome had made him an industry player and he also had a reputation for opportunistic hits built around popular characters from TV series. However, it's fair to say that outside the industry, few people had heard of Cowell. He was well off and successful, certainly, but a long way short of achieving the fame and multi-million pound fortune of today.

His association with Simon Fuller was to change all that.

DIVIDE THE SPOILS

Cowell and Fuller worked together on the format for *Pop Idol*, a show that would make both men rich and Cowell very famous indeed. The idea certainly wasn't new. In 2000, Cowell was asked by TV producer Nigel Lythgoe to appear as a judge on soon to be aired talent show *Popstars*. Cowell turned it down but when the show turned out to be success, he and Simon Fuller began talks on a similar series.

Fuller and Cowell were in many respects ideal partners. Both had achieved success within the industry and both were unashamedly in the business of developing talent for the mainstream pop market. What's more, their biographies showed a certain amount of overlap.

In common with Cowell, Fuller's first real job in the entertainment industry was as an A&R man at a record company, the relatively small and innovative Chrysalis label. He had success early when he signed musician and writer Paul Hardcastle who went on to take his song '19' to the top of the charts in 1985.

'19' was very far from a conventional pop hit. Drawing on dance music and hip hop it was themed around the fact that the average

age of soldiers serving in Vietnam was 19. The record caught the mood of the times and sold well around the world. The money it made for Fuller enabled him to set up his own company, 19 Entertainment.

Fuller moved on from A&R into management and up until *Pop Idol*, he was probably best known as the man behind the success of the Spice Girls. Under Fuller's management, the feisty all-girl singing group took the British charts by storm when their debut single 'Wannabe' went to number one in the charts in 1996. The following year it achieved the same position in the US. Their debut album sold something in the region of 23m.

Waterman's profile as a music industry mogul has been long eclipsed by that of Cowell, but it's widely accepted that he played a huge role in getting the younger man's career out of second gear.

Formed in 1994, the band signed with Fuller's company a year later and stayed with him until 1997. Despite the relatively short working relationship, Fuller can justifiably claim to have steered the group through their most lucrative period. It wasn't just a case of selling records. Fuller – like Cowell – is a great believer in maximizing revenue potential – in addition to cash from record sales and personal appearances, the group also benefitted from sponsorship deals with the likes of Pepsi, Impulse and Polaroid.

Cowell considered the Spice Girls for S Records at a time when they were still looking for a deal, so he and Fuller were clearly on each other's radar screens at that point, even though it was Virgin who ultimately signed the band. In retrospect there seemed to be a real affinity. Cowell has since likened Fuller to a 'brother'. In professional terms both careers have been characterized by competitive ambition and a willingness to experiment with new ways to market music.

The partnership between Cowell and Fuller really began in 2000 when they agreed to collaborate on a TV show that would build on the success of *Popstars*. The deal they struck reflected their positions within the industry. Fuller's management company 19 Entertainment would own the rights to the show and he would manage the winners. Cowell, the record industry man, would not have any ownership over the show itself but he, on behalf of BMG Records, would have the right to sign the artists who appeared.

In other words, the deal gave both men a piece of the action. With the 20/20 vision of hindsight you could argue that Fuller got the biggest slice. Fuller's ownership of the rights to *Pop Idol* – and its successful *American Idol* counterpart – gave him a powerful platform on which to grow 19 Entertainment and he went on to sell the company for $151m cash, plus $1.9m in shares to CFX in 2005.

But Cowell hasn't done too badly either. In the UK, *Pop Idol* discovered Gareth Gates and Will Young in its first season, delivering not one but two talented singers to Cowell and BMG. *American Idol* established Cowell as a TV star with massive earnings potential in the US market.

Prior to announcing a decision to quit *American Idol* in 2010 he secured a £22m a year payment from Fox TV. Perhaps more importantly, Cowell's continued presence on the show gave him leverage when the time came to launch his own shows – notably *America's Got Talent* and *American Inventor* – in the US market.

So you could argue that the Cowell/Fuller alliance was a marriage made in heaven. According to one of the golden rules of successful partnerships, each of the two men had his own sphere of influence (management and TV production for Fuller, record sales and fame for Cowell) so both got a decent share of the proceeds.

But the partnership hasn't stood the test of time without some bumps and bangs. Cowell played a significant role in the planning and execution of *Pop Idol*, so it is perhaps natural that his thoughts ultimately turned to a bigger slice of the pie. In 2005, Fuller and Cowell found themselves on opposite sides of the courtroom when Cowell's Syco launched *X Factor* in the UK in association with TV production companies Fremantle Media and Thames Talkback. Fuller cried foul, claiming he had identified 25 similarities between the new show and *Pop Idol*, an accusation lying at the heart of a breach of copyright case that ultimately resulted in an out-of-court settlement.

The details of the agreement weren't disclosed but what we do know is that Cowell continued to be a judge on *American Idol* while *X Factor* went on to eclipse *Pop Idol* in the UK. The friendship, if not the partnership between Cowell and Fuller apparently survived. 'I suppose we're like brothers, and brothers squabble,' Cowell told the *FT*. 'We're incredibly competitive and always have been, so it was probably inevitable that at some point during *Idol* that we would split up because we're too similar.'[2]

PUT BUSINESS FIRST

The partnership between Cowell and Fuller is not the only one to have been put under strain by the competitive pressures of television. If media reports are to be believed, Cowell's long-term association with pop music manager and stalwart of *X Factor* Louis Walsh has also taken its fair share of punishment.

Walsh is a product of the Irish music scene and has gone on to secure international success with his management of boy band acts Boyzone and Westlife.

He began his career in music working for a showband promotions company. On the face of it, that's a pretty inauspicious start. Showbands are essentially covers bands by another name. They tour the country playing the chart songs of the day and while the bigger names have had hit records in their own right they are essentially there to replicate music that the audience already knows from radio and TV. But in a country that loves live music, showbands flourished in the post war years and the bigger names could pack out sizeable venues. Working as a showband promoter gave Walsh a good grounding in the industry.

Each of the two men had his own sphere of influence (management and TV production for Fuller, record sales and fame for Cowell) and spoils were divided.

His association with Simon Cowell began with Westlife. Walsh was already an industry 'name' by this time, having discovered Boyzone. Working out of Dublin he was able to persuade Cowell to take a short hop across the Irish Sea to give his latest discoveries the once over. Cowell was unconvinced, advising Walsh to make line up changes. Walsh settled for an image makeover and after seeing them for a second time Cowell signed the band. They became one of his biggest selling acts.

Walsh was something of a natural choice for *X Factor*. He had a recognized track record and, like Cowell, he had an eye and ear for the elements that add up to make a hit record. He also had some experience in the world of reality/talent contest TV having sat on the judging panel for the Irish version of *Popstars*. The transition from Irish to British TV was an easy one and, once ensconced in the *X Factor* studio, he made a good foil to fellow judges Cowell and Sharon Osbourne.

Sparks often flew, though. Rivalry between the judges was built into the DNA of the show. By creating a situation where each judge mentors a group of performers, Cowell ensured that each member of the panel had professional interests in seeing their own acts do well as the knockout stage of the show progressed. This has had the effect of creating a doubled-edged competition. If the competitors are up against each other, so are the judges.

Tabloid newspapers love the spats and bust ups between the *X Factor* judges. For outsiders though, it is hard to know how much of the rivalry is real and how much is concocted for the camera. What we do know is that Walsh quit the show in 2007, citing poor treatment by the other judges. He vowed never to return.

But he did. Signing on for Series 5 in 2008 and presumably welcomed by Cowell. If there's a lesson here it is that personal issues can be overcome if it is to the benefit of both partners.

CAST YOUR NET WIDER

Given Cowell's growing wealth and power within the media industry, it would be surprising if he didn't seek commercial partnerships beyond the worlds of television and music. After all, he is now recognized not simply as a music/TV mogul but as one of the UK's most successful men. His peers are no longer his colleagues in the entertainment world but successful businessmen of all stripes – and presumably often pin stripes.

Witness Cowell's association with Peter Jones. Jones is a self-made millionaire who made his fortune in the mobile phone, telecom and new media fields while latterly finding fame as a judge on *Dragons' Den*. *Dragons' Den* is the BBC's upmarket reality TV show in which hopeful entrepreneurs pitch their ideas to a panel of investors who are prepared to pump hard cash into business plans that win their approval.

Jones and Cowell became partners in developing and producing the television series *American Inventor*, aired on ABC in the US. The show was conceived by Jones and when it was turned down by the BBC, he struck a deal with Cowell to have it produced by Syco, Fremantle Media and Peter Jones TV.

The format would be recognizable to followers of *X Factor*, *American Idol* or *Dragons' Den*. The aim of the show was to find an inventor with a concept that could go on to become a marketable product. Winners in each episode received cash to develop their ideas and a place in the later stages of the competition. The overall prize was $1m. To date, *Inventor* hasn't been given a third series.

According to the *Financial Times*, Jones and Cowell hit it off immediately – agreeing to work together after only one meeting. Perhaps that's not surprising. The two men appear to share a belief that blunt honesty is the best policy. Like Cowell, Jones has earned something of a reputation for no-holds-barred put-downs of *Dragons' Den* contestants that he takes exception to. His justification is similar to that of Cowell's. 'I like to think of myself as Mr Honest,' he told the *FT*, 'It aggravates me when you have a complete lunatic appearing on the programme. The guy is wasting my time and I have to sit there for half an hour.'[3]

Or it could have been shared experience that broke the ice. Like Cowell, Jones has seen hard times, losing his fortune when an early business venture went bust. Like many entrepreneurs, he climbed back to his feet and started again, becoming even more successful.

Cowell's partnership is not one that would raise many eyebrows. While the two men come from very different business backgrounds – Jones majoring in telecoms while Cowell is steeped in entertainment – they are both well-known television personalities. In their respective shows the roles they play are not dissimilar. The on-screen Jones applies his commercial know-how to damn or praise the presentations of would-be entrepreneurs while Cowell brings to bear his own particular brand of *savoir-faire* when judging pop hopefuls.

And of course, Cowell and Jones are much more than screen presences. As commercially minded individuals both have understood the commercial opportunities inherent in TV production. Both own their own production companies. In other words, they swim in overlapping seas even though their origins are different.

Arguably more surprising is Cowell's association with retail magnate Sir Philip Green.

At first sight, Green and Cowell appear to be polar opposites. Cowell is a relaxed, T-shirt wearing product of the music industry, whilst Green is an old-school British businessman, much more at home in boardrooms than studio green rooms.

Green started his first business at the age of 15 when he began to import jeans from the Far East to sell on to retailers. Since then he has ascended through the ranks of Britain's wealthiest businessmen, often via a strategy of acquiring retail businesses and reselling them at a profit. For instance, in the early 1990s, he bought department store chain Owen Owen, and over a period of time sold the individual branches to other retailers at a profit. He also secured financial backing to buy the Sears retail organization for a hefty £538m, which he then resold over time at a profit. He has now become a dominant figure on the British High Street.

His world seems a million miles away from the universe occupied by Cowell both in terms of its business models and culture. Scratch below the surface though and the two businesses aren't entirely dissimilar. Whether the product is a boy band or a summer top, it's all about taking a product, adding value, marketing and turning a profit. Nor is the wheeling and dealing poles apart. Green has built a retail empire, Cowell (albeit with the backing of Sony) has constructed a business that operates across media. Along the way, both men have done their share of bargaining.

Given Cowell's growing wealth and power within the media industry, it would be surprising if he didn't seek commercial partnerships.

If you're going to establish a commercial relationship there really has to be something in it for both partners. After all you can be friends and discuss respective business plans over dinner, at a golf club or in the back of a taxi. But when you announce a commercial relationship, then there has to be the prospect of a pay day.

So what lies behind the relationship between Cowell and Green?

In 2009 Cowell and Green announced plans to set up a company that would hold the rights of Cowell's existing assets, including *X Factor* and the *Got Talent* franchise, and develop new formats for the sale of these assets around the world.

The announcement came at a crucial time for Cowell. His contract to appear as a judge on *American Idol* was coming up for renewal as was his contract to run Syco on behalf of Sony. Against this background, the partnership with Green was seen as increasing Cowell's negotiating muscle ahead of the contractual talks.

Arguably this was of particular concern to Sony. Since joining BMG (prior to its takeover by Sony) Cowell had worked under the wing of a major entertainment company and his success at Syco had been underpinned by a corporate backer. In theory at least, an association with a financial heavyweight could give him a lot more independence in terms of developing and marketing his television and music formats. There was speculation that Cowell would break away from Sony and even suggestions – quickly quashed – that he and Green might launch a bid for ITV.

The deal with Sony means Cowell once again has ownership (in part) of the Syco operation.

Meanwhile, if the *Financial Times*[4] was to be believed, the newly forged partnership represented an opportunity for Philip Green to market his clothing brands through Cowell's TV and music industry interests. That aspect of the agreement was supported by reports that fashion model Kate Moss was to join the partnership as a figurehead for the fashion retailing side of the business.

It remains to be seen how the Cowell/Green company – now dubbed Greenwell Entertainment will pan out. In 2010, Cowell successfully renegotiated his contract with Sony. In place of the previous deal, with the record company owning 100% of Syco, the new arrangement sees the creation of a 50/50 joint venture with Sony and Cowell having an equal stake in the business. Confirming the deal, Sony Music Entertainment welcomed a continuing partnership. 'Over the past 20 years, Simon Cowell has been a great partner and is an integral part of the Sony Music global family. We are extremely excited to be able to continue and further develop our relationship with Simon, and significantly grow the Syco venture',[5] said Rolf Schmidt-Holtz, the company's CEO.

The deal with Sony means Cowell once again has ownership (in part) of the Syco operation while parting with Fox is likely to see him launching a concerted attack on the US market with *X Factor* and other formats. If the partnership continues, Green is likely to be a formidable ally in Cowell's bid to expand his TV empire.

Partnership is a way of life in the entertainment industry. Big labels work with independent producers. TV companies buy from independent production houses. Managers work with record companies and television producers to promote their artists. Cowell is undoubtedly a mover and shaker, but well chosen partnerships have been instrumental to his success.

WORK WITH PARTNERS

Cowell has collaborated successfully with a number of key partners over the years. This is how he's made it work.

- **Divide the spoils.** In any business deal it's important to ensure that all parties get something substantial from the agreement. When Cowell worked with Simon Fuller on *Pop Idol* the spoils were divided. Fuller's 19 Entertainment owned the show, but Cowell got first pick of the artists for his record label. He was well paid by both ITV and later by Fox for his role as judge on *American Idol*. Less directly, the success of *American Idol* gave him a power base in the US that he is currently seeking to exploit to the full.

- **Put business first.** Cowell's creation of *X Factor* for the UK market created a real strain in his relationship with Simon Fuller, with the latter taking court action over similarities between the two shows. Nevertheless, an out-of-court settlement was reached and Cowell continued to work on the Fuller-owned *American Idol*. Like many businessmen in such circumstances, it appears that Cowell and Fuller chose a mutually beneficial compromise.

- **Cast your net wider.** Cowell has looked beyond the entertainment industry for partners, working with telecoms millionaire Peter Jones on *American Inventor* (ABC network). More recently he has teamed up with retail magnate Sir Philip Green to create a global company to exploit Cowell's existing assets and develop new formats. From the retailer's point of view, Cowell's television assets represent a channel to promote his fashion products. Like all good partnerships, both sides get something out of it.

7

TELL IT LIKE IT IS

'But I wasn't in his league when it came to directness. Simon was, and is, so focused. I've never been that ruthless.'[1]

– Pete Waterman, record producer

'I DON'T MEAN TO BE RUDE BUT ...'

It's the well-worn phrase dreaded by every contestant on *X Factor*, *American Idol* or *Britain's Got Talent*. Inevitably those seven short words are the preface to a put-down intended to sink any misguided hopes of a career in the music business or entertainment industry. For those who sing tunelessly, dance without rhythm or tell jokes that leave the audience cringing rather than laughing, Cowell is a pocket battleship piled high with deadly verbal shells. Perform badly within his line of sight and he'll blow you out of the water.

Try this for size. 'Let me throw a mathematical dilemma at you. There's 500 left [in the competition] so how come the odds of you winning are a million to one.' Or this: 'You have just invented a new form of torture.'[2]

You get the picture. After almost a decade of appearances on *X Factor*, *Pop Idol*, *American Idol* and *Britain's Got Talent*, Cowell has probably committed thousands of put-downs to video tape. Some are ornate and witty, others blunt and to the point. Most leave the hopes of the recipients lying in tatters. And it's not only the contestants who feel the sharp end of his tongue. He is also noted for verbally roughing up his fellow judges. It's all good knockabout stuff that keeps the viewers coming back for more.

And for many people, that's where Simon Cowell begins and ends. He is a sharp-tongued, edgy entertainer who doesn't suffer fools gladly. His legendary capacity for plain speaking has elevated him to a position somewhere between national treasure and Mr Nasty.

But of course, we all know there's a lot more to Cowell than the man we see on screen. Behind the façade of the pantomime villain there is a businessman with a multi-million pound fortune, someone who is, according to those who know him, a nice guy who is generous and fun to be with.

But you can't really separate Cowell's on-screen persona from his success. For one thing, his personal style – edgy, pugnacious, plain speaking – has become a personal brand and, by extension, a vital component in the branding of his TV shows. Love or hate *X Factor*, you have to admit that the Cowell personality gives the show an edge. The other judges play their part, but ultimately it is Cowell that the public is tuning in to see.

Dig a little deeper and it's not hard to forge a link between the entertainer we see on screen and the successful businessman. The tendency towards plain speaking is just one aspect of the man. Watch him on TV and you see a lot of other things going on as well. There is the supreme self-confidence of someone whose default position appears to be 'I am right about everything.' Equally important, there is a steely determination to get what he wants coupled with a restless competiveness. As *X Factor* runs its course, Cowell fights tooth and claw for the competitors he has opted to mentor. When the show ends and the hit making machine takes over, he does what it takes to ensure he has the Christmas number one.

Restlessness, competitiveness, and a determination to do your own thing even if it means breaking rules are all admirable qualities for someone with an entrepreneurial frame of mind. They can be a lot less appropriate – indeed a real disadvantage – in the world of school or the corporate workplace.

So let's step back a bit and look at the bigger picture. These qualities can be seen as defining factors in Cowell's career. Even at school he was determined to do things his own way, even if that meant little more than smoking, drinking and letting his grades slip. So how did Cowell – the boy who was expelled from one school and left another with just two O levels – turn his life around? How did a restless young man who attended numerous fruitless job interviews before taking on a lowly post-room job at EMI records climb his way to the top? To what extent was his uncompromising character a factor in his ascent? In the world of work, he quickly demonstrated ambition coupled with an independence of mind. Witness his rapid departure from employer EMI to set up an independent record label (E&S) with Ellis Rich. And as his career developed, he acquired a reputation as someone prepared to speak his mind, even when challenging conventional wisdom.

FIND THE RIGHT INDUSTRY

The Cowell paradox is that for all his iconoclasm he has worked within corporate structures through a lot of his career. EMI, BMG, Sony – these are all big name companies employing thousands of people, just like BP, KPMG or British Gas.

But arguably, Cowell chose his industry well. The record business, unlike say accountancy or the chemicals industry – is celebrated for its mavericks. People who work within or alongside a corporate structure while cutting their own path through the world. Put simply, it's a world where talent earns you a lot of slack.

The mavericks don't necessarily make it to the top of the tree, if the pinnacle is defined as, say, the CEO's job in a major record label such as EMI or Sony. Cowell's strategy over the years has often been to establish a power base within a larger organization as the boss of an independent production house. For instance, when he joined BMG as an A&R consultant, he formed S Records within the group. Later, with an increasingly successful television career, he formed

Syco Records as a vehicle through which to develop TV shows and market records promoted by those shows. Syco has since had a bit of a chequered history. Owned initially by Cowell, it was later sold to Sony. Since 2010 it has been operating as a 50/50, Cowell/Sony joint venture.

Running an autonomous unit within a larger group or with the backing of a major organization is arguably the ideal situation for a maverick. On the one hand, you have the financial support that a relationship with a big company can provide. Meanwhile, you can get on with running the business the way you want to run it, provided you make money for your parent.

His legendary capacity for plain speaking has elevated him to a position somewhere between national treasure and Mr Nasty.

In latter years, Cowell has had no trouble on the moneymaking front. S Records had a string of hits and Syco – with its multi media interests in CDs, downloads, TV and video – has made the parent company millions. Back in 2006, Cowell famously claimed that Syco was responsible for 40% of Sony UK's profits, despite having just 15 members of staff.[3]

And while Syco is a moneymaking machine for Sony, it has also given Cowell the profile he currently enjoys. The company is responsible for producing *X Factor* and *Britain's Got Talent*, and Cowell calls the shots. Appearing on those programmes enhances his personal brand, and his own status as a TV ratings driver has given him a huge amount of power within the industry.

Cowell's autonomy didn't come easily. In the early years of his career, he nearly ran aground when he left EMI to form E&S Records with Ellis Rich. The company went on to have chart success but not before Cowell had left – disillusioned – in search of other things. His next partnership – with Iain Burton, founder of Fanfare Records – was more successful. Acting in the role of A&R man, Cowell notched up hits with Sinitta and others. By the time the company folded under the pressure of debts, Cowell had an industry track record. When he subsequently joined BMG and set up S Records, he had evidence of success behind him. That success gave him a power base.

CREATE A PERSONAL BRAND

We live in the age of the brand. From the clothes we wear to the computers we use for work and play, we make choices determined not just by cost, style and build quality but also the 'brand values' that underpin those products.

Increasingly we're seeing that the concept of the brand extends to people. Business owners have long recognized the power of the personal brand when it comes to shifting product. Arguably Virgin would be a much less successful business empire if it wasn't underpinned by Richard Branson's own personal brand. And Branson is by no means unique. From lifestyle empress Martha Stewart to streetwise chef Jamie Oliver, strong personal brands can supercharge product sales. If we trust the individual and like or respect what they stand for, we are more likely to buy into what they have to sell.

The same broad principles of personal branding apply in the job market and the workplace. At its simplest, your personal brand is how you are perceived by others. In a professional context that perception can affect your promotion chances, the type of work that you're given or the likelihood of an application standing out from those of other applicants when you send a CV to a prospective employer.

The brand is the sum total of a lot of professional and personal factors. It is not only what you are in terms of qualifications, experience and your skill sets but also who you are – team player or loner; leader or deputy; a stickler for tried and tested procedures or blue sky thinker.

The key to personal branding is to ensure that the face you show to friends and colleagues chimes with your ambitions. So if your goal is to become a project manager dealing with the senior management of blue chip companies on a day-to-day basis then it's vital that your brand is aligned with that ambition.

Restlessness, competitiveness, and a determination to do your own thing are all admirable qualities for someone with an entrepreneurial frame of mind.

But you've got to keep it real. The key element in developing a personal brand is authenticity. You can certainly cultivate your brand – accentuating those parts of your personality that are most helpful in the workplace – but it shouldn't be fabricated. At root the brand should reflect your personality. If it doesn't you'll soon be found out.

One of Cowell's major achievements is to brand himself as a plain speaking, music business expert who shoots from the hip and is cruel to be kind. It's a brand that has certainly been developed during his time in front of the cameras but it is nonetheless authentic. Forthright speaking is part of his personality.

Most of us learn to think before we speak in the workplace. It's not rocket science. When a superior asks for an opinion on his or her latest plan to boost productivity, to increase profits and reduce waste, we'll tend to put a positive spin on our answer, even if we think the scheme harebrained and unworkable. When your boss asks for feedback, stark honesty isn't really what is expected.

The same principle tends to apply when dealing with co-workers. Acid comment about the standard of a colleague's work doesn't tend to go down too well, even if other people secretly agree. And even in formal exercises such as appraisals, any negative feedback about an individual's work tends to be couched in ultra diplomatic terms. Indeed, there are occasions when a negative report on an individual's work becomes so watered down that it is indistinguishable from a commendation.

Running an autonomous unit within a larger group is arguably the ideal situation for a maverick.

In short, most of us tend to bite our tongues. It's easier that way. Quieter. We don't make enemies and (in terms of our relationships with those above us in the food chain) we don't generate waves.

Those in charge don't operate under the same constraints. When you run the show, you can say what you like and no one's going to argue. That's not to say all bosses take advantage of a licence to be rude or abrasive – that tends to be counterproductive – but Cowell is certainly among those who seem to believe it is better to speak your mind than let an individual go on believing that he's doing a good job when he clearly isn't. In the Cowell Gospel, plain speaking can only be a good thing.

It's a principle that is writ large across the Cowell TV persona. Cowell has absolutely no compunction in telling a performer that he or she is completely lacking in talent. It is, he argues, a kindness of sorts. 'You cannot survive in this business unless you know when you've made a mistake', he told the Hollyscoop website in May 2008, 'So I would feel guilty about giving people fake hope when I genuinely believe they have no chance.'[4]

There's undoubtedly a huge amount of truth in that argument. The bulk of people who turn up for talent show auditions have no chance of pursuing a career in the music industry. Some undoubtedly know that and are simply there to get on TV. Others clearly don't and as executioner-in-chief, Cowell is there to set them straight before they waste too much of their lives chasing a fruitless dream.

There is, of course, a question mark over that defence. On the shows he takes part in, Cowell is just one of a panel of judges. All of them regularly serve up negative feedback to contestants but seldom with the same amount of verbal dexterity mixed with acid that Cowell seems to effortlessly conjure up. Put simply, the other judges are generally nicer at saying no to the hopeless and the hapless.

But the degree of moderation or self censorship shown by the judges simply throws Cowell's persona into sharp relief. We see the others prevaricating, beating round the bush or thinking carefully before giving a contestant bad news. Cowell simply wades in with the truth (as he sees it).

Cowell has knowingly built on aspects of his character that were already in place to create the persona that we see on-screen. He is a dominant presence and everything revolves around him. 'Every week he does or says something that makes him more famous, and that's all he wants ... that's what drives him,' record producer and long time friend and associate Pete Waterman told the *Daily Telegraph*.[5]

Arguably then, Cowell has reached a point in his career that is uniquely suited to the restless teenager who had no time for school rules and yet was hungry for financial success. He has shaped his own reality, running companies in which he calls the shots. What's more, he has turned what could have been a handicap into a virtue. His willingness to speak his mind whenever a camera or reporter's notebook is at hand has endeared him to the nation. To an extent at least, he says the inconvenient or politically incorrect things that many of us are thinking but don't dare to utter. And we love him for it. He is an iconoclast and a one-off and even if we don't always share his opinions, we enjoy it when he expresses them.

This in turn gives him even more power to do things his way. As long as his personality helps *X Factor*, *American Idol* and the *Got Talent* programmes to stay at the top of ratings, he will be a powerful player in the entertainment industry.

That's brand Simon – the entertainer we see on TV. So what about businessman Simon? Does the same plain speaking style work in the world of commerce?

MAKE HONESTY THE BEST POLICY

The first thing that has to be said is that Cowell's on-screen persona is just that – a construct designed to hold the attention of viewers over the weeks and months of a series. In the real world, away from the camera, it's unlikely that he spends his waking hours aiming perfectly honed put-downs at friends, colleagues and business partners.

However, he is a firm believer that honesty – and that includes blunt honesty – is by far the best policy when doing business. As he told the *Daily Mail* in 2009, it was a lesson he learned from mentor Pete Waterman. 'If I'm ever cruel, it's because show business is cruel … I learned much over the years, from people like Pete Waterman – real tough love. He once said to me, "You don't know what you're talking about … Come back when you've got a hit." I took it as a challenge.'[6]

That's where Cowell's on-screen personality overlaps with the real life man. He knows what he wants and he's prepared to say so upfront. He doesn't beat about the bush and he doesn't waste time with those who don't see things his way.

That's where Cowell's on-screen personality overlaps with the real life man. He knows what he wants and he's prepared to say so upfront.

Writer Chas Newkey-Burden provides an illustration of this in his book *Simon Cowell: the unauthorized biography*. The first series of *Pop Idol* produced two stars from Cowell's label in the shape of Will Young and Gareth Gates. There might have been a third. Cowell was keen to sign contestant Darius Danesh. Cowell had a clear game plan. Danesh would record a cover version of a well known song – 'You've lost that loving feeling' – and ride to the top of the charts on the surf of his *Pop Idol* fame. Danesh, on the other hand, wanted to record his own songs. As Newkey-Burden puts it 'he got short shrift' and he chose to turn down the deal on offer.[7]

Such encounters are part and parcel of life in the music industry, particularly in Cowell's own field of production line pop. As someone experienced in masterminding hit records, Cowell knows his business and he isn't going to be deflected from what he believes is commercially right by the ambitions of a singer whose plans run counter to his own. Where some might deal in ambiguity to get the singer to sign for the label and come on board, Cowell is upfront. In these circumstances honesty is the best way to stay fully in control of the ship.

It's not a management style that suits everyone. According to a survey by Britain's Chartered Institute of Management (CMI), 12% of the UK workforce find the rough-hewn upfront management style – as exemplified on TV by Cowell and Alan Sugar – to be a turn off.

Cowell's capacity for blunt plain speaking is underpinned by his A&R savvy.

But there are plenty of others who see his upfront style as a refreshing antidote to the norm in a great many organizations where managers are reluctant to say what they think – and by extension reluctant to manage.

Once such advocate of the Cowell style is Dan McGinn, a *Harvard Business Review* editor. Writing on the *Review*'s blog he had this to say about the Cowell approach: 'I've always thought Cowell's style, while over-the-top, is relevant for managers … Yes, he's unnecessarily mean and nasty – hey, it's a TV show – but he's also one of the world's foremost practitioners of a word that pops up in *HBR* every so often: candor.'[8]

As McGinn goes on to point out, lack of candor in a working environment can be a corrosive thing. The employee who thinks he or she is doing well at particular job may in fact be failing and because no one is prepared to be honest and upfront, the likelihood is that their performance will continue to be the norm. In the short term, the employee carries on as usual. In the longer term, he or she could be first in line for redundancy when the organization decides that it's time to downsize.

But the truth is that upfront honesty can be a hard quality to muster. That's especially true in the modern workplace where the emphasis is often on team building and a collegiate approach to doing business. Managers – particularly middle managers – who work closely with team members on a day-to-day basis often find it difficult to criticize individuals that they are personally close to.

But it is a necessary skill. Few things undermine group morale more than individuals within a team failing to pull their weight. Equally, a failure to deal with this kind of issue will certainly undermine the manager's authority and standing within the group. So in McGinn's view the workplace could do with less politeness and a little more of the directness shown by Cowell.

But it's important to remember that Cowell's directness doesn't exist in a vacuum. If he was simply being rude to contestants for the sake of it, there would be little merit in his approach. But Cowell's capacity for blunt speaking is underpinned by his A&R savvy. He knows what his audience wants and he has an eye and ear for performers who will appeal to his target consumer. He has a strong track record in matching those performers with songs that have the potential to become major hits. In short, he has earned the right to take what some would see as a didactic view of what constitutes a good singer or a hit song.

You could argue that – on TV at least – Cowell's 'honest' assessments of singers and the performers is informed by a narrow view of what is and isn't good. His shows and his label seem to have no time or space for edgy artists offering self-written songs and an original approach to performance. You couldn't imagine the younger Cowell recognizing the talent of a young Bob Dylan, a John Lennon or even a Noel Gallagher. Even in his chosen battlefield of mainstream pop his judgment isn't unerring. Cowell turned down Take That, arguably the most enduring of the boy bands to emerge in the 1990s, and almost passed on Westlife.

But the fact remains that within his pure pop niche he has provided ample evidence of the ability to spot talent and good songs. Despite mistakes of Take That proportions, his track record has earned him the right to do things his own way. If Cowell likes you, thinks you have potential and signs you to his label, he'll do everything in his power to make your records successful. But his opinion holds sway. He tells it like it is and how it's going to be.

KNOW YOUR LIMITATIONS

Cowell is not so forthright when outside his comfort zone. At least that's a view expressed by Mark Hoffman, a property developer who is in partnership with Cowell and his brother Nicholas.

Hoffman's business was set up in 2005 to buy and sell properties in the UK and, according to the *Jewish Chronicle*, the company's first deal – the development of a vacant site in Commercial Road – was funded by a £1m investment from Cowell. In an interview with the paper, Hoffman paints a picture of a Cowell that we don't often hear about; as someone who is willing to take a back seat as those better qualified than him go about their business: 'He doesn't pretend to be an expert in things that he's not … he very much goes on our advice.'[9]

However, while Cowell is for the most part hands-off, he is certainly not detached from the decisions made by Hoffman and Nicholas Cowell. Hoffman describes him as a stickler for detail who can be demanding: 'If we say we are going to do something, he will expect it to be done.'

Since leaving school at fifteen, Cowell has evolved from an adolescent boy whose career prospects were apparently blighted by an inability or unwillingness to buckle down, into a flamboyant leader who knows exactly what he wants and speaks his mind firmly and clearly. Something that was an apparent weakness has – in the right circumstances – revealed itself as a strength. What's more, his bluntness is a character trait ideally suited to the needs of reality TV and is now part of his brand.

TELL IT LIKE IT IS

Honesty in the workplace – or indeed in any situation – can be a double-edged sword. Being straight with people is considered a quality, but in the wrong circumstances it can cause a huge amount of offence. In the workplace, those who speak out of turn (or without first thinking carefully about what they have to say) can find their careers blighted.

And yet Simon Cowell has made a virtue out of his 'tell it like it is' personality. Uncomfortable with rules and regulations, he's forged an individual path through his chosen industry.

- **Find the right industry.** Cowell left EMI to work in executive positions in two small record companies. In the second – Fanfare – he achieved significant success before the parent company collapsed under the weight of its debts. When he returned to the corporate world – in the shape of BMG records – he set up his own label within the company. With a degree of autonomy he was able to pursue his own strategy for having hit records. In the music business Cowell chose an industry where mavericks are welcome, provided of course they can demonstrate a track record of success.

- **Create a personal brand.** In the parlance of the career consultant, we should all have a personal brand. Essentially our brand is how people see us and how we want to be seen and it's important that the image we present to the world is aligned with our ambitions. Cowell's brand is that of the straight talking, no-bullshit manager who tells it like it is. It's a brand that he's developed to perfection under the glare of the television lights. It's also authentic, reflecting his off-screen self, albeit in enhanced form. Authenticity is key when developing a personal brand.

- **Make honesty the best policy.** Cowell believes honesty – even brutal honesty – is kinder than allowing those on the receiving end of his candor to wallow in self-delusion. On TV that often means acid put-downs of hopeful contestants on his talent/reality shows. Cowell extends that principle off-screen. He may not be showboating for the camera but is noted for being absolutely clear about what he wants from those working for him. It's a skill that is lacking in many managers who are reluctant to offend or upset those they work with. However, failure to speak out when you think an employee or colleague is not performing well can store up problems for the long term. If someone doesn't know there is a problem he or she won't be able to address it.

- **Know your limitations**. Away from the industry he knows – entertainment – Cowell is prepared to play a hands-off role and take advice from others. However, he will question his business partners very closely to ensure he knows what is going on and to ascertain everyone involved is doing what needs to be done.

8

MANAGE THE TALENT

'I'm just trying to point these people in a more credible career path for themselves because, you know, we've had half a million people apply on *American Idol* over five seasons. To date, we've launched two, maybe three careers, so this is after all that TV exposure.'[1]

– Simon Cowell

AND THE WINNER IS ...

It's the moment that viewers have been awaiting for months. The results of the phone votes have been counted and the compère is about to reveal the name of the victorious contestant. When the announcement is made, there will be cheers, tears, standing ovations and garbled words of thanks. Meanwhile, Simon Cowell and his fellow judges prepare to congratulate the winner and commiserate with those who failed to make the top spot. Another series of *X Factor* is coming to an end.

In the fickle world of the entertainment industry, some of the winners may enjoy little more than a few years – or even months – in the limelight before they return to the real world of jobs or low-profile bookings in small clubs. And as their stars fade, Cowell and his team will be shepherding a new band of hopefuls on the torturous road from open auditions to finals. New winners will take the stage. And even if last year's champion fades quickly into obscurity, leaving little more than a footnote in pop history, there will always be more candidates in the pipeline. Individual careers may rise and fall but Cowell, the businessman, will continue to ring up hit after hit after hit.

This doesn't mean that Cowell doesn't care about the artists he signs to his label on the strength of a strong outing on *X Factor* or *Britain's Got Talent*. A talented singer who can forge a long-term career as a big selling artist is worth more to Syco Records than a one-off flash in the pan. Talented, bankable singers are an asset.

Cowell doesn't always get it right but he has a good track record in working with artists in the medium and longer term. Sitting within the Syco stable are acts such as Westlife and Il Divo who've worked with Cowell over many years – indeed since well before the arrival of *X Factor* on UK screens. Shayne Ward, *X Factor*'s first winner, is still signed to the label and the 2006 winner, Leona Lewis, has established herself as an international star in the Whitney Houston/soul diva mould.

So clearly *X Factor* winners are not simply throwaways. Those who have real potential have every chance of carving out good careers. So let's take a closer look at how Cowell manages the talent.

KEEP THE CONTRACTS TIGHT

Cowell's ability to milk the best possible return from artists signed through talent shows screened in the UK and around the world depends first and foremost on the hopeful participants signing watertight contracts.

Under normal circumstances the contract details would be confidential, with the details known only to Sony, Syco, the contestants and sundry lawyers, but back in December 2008, details of a document relating to *X Factor* were leaked to the press.

As far as the newspapers were concerned, the key revelation concerned the supposed differential between the headline prize for a winner of *X Factor* and the actual amount of money on the table. It's part of the mythology of the show that winners walk away with a deal worth £1m but as the *Daily Mirror*[2] and the *Independent*[3] noted, the documentation made clear that the victorious finalist would not simply be handed a cheque for a cool million.

In fact, the money was broken down into tranches, with the winner initially receiving a £150,000 advance against sales. So where did that nice round figure of £1m come from?

What the *X Factor* winner receives is not a cash prize but a fairly standard industry contract. In addition to giving the signee cash up front, the company will also be spending on advertising, video shoots, photo shoots and all the other essential pieces of work that go hand and hand with going into a studio and making a record, which is where the value lies.

As the leaks revealed, it didn't mean that the victorious finalist would simply be handed a cheque for a cool million.

Commenting on the leak, Sony was unrepentant. 'The prize for winning *The X Factor* is a recording contract with Sony BMG. The value of recording an album can be around or in some cases, far in excess of £1m and *The X Factor* contract is a standard recording contract,'[4] the company said in a statement.

In reality, nobody should have been surprised by the breakdown of the contract. More interesting was what the leaked document revealed about the contractual ties binding Cowell and Syco to the competitors.

As things stood, competitors in the show were given three weeks to decide whether or not to sign the contract that would enable them to participate in the show and had the right to take legal advice at Cowell's expense.

The contract allowed Cowell first bite of the cherry on all the acts appearing on *X Factor*. The outright winner of the show was guaranteed that '£1m' deal, while the other competitors were required to agree to remain under contract to Syco for at least three months after the final. This allowed Cowell and his team time to weigh up their potential and pick up on the option of signing them to a record deal. While the winner got an advance of £150,000, the others could expect more modest upfront payments.

Artists signed by Cowell would find they didn't have much control over their career direction as under the terms of the contract, Sony had the final say on any tracks recorded. There wasn't much control on the management front either. The contract made it clear that winners would be required to join Modest! Management. No other choice of manager would be available.

Meanwhile, competitors who didn't make it onto Syco weren't quite free of contractual obligations. Those who went on to forge their own careers in show business agreed to pay Cowell's organization 5% of their live earnings for up to a year.

Little of this was particularly draconian. The advance figures quoted for winners and runners-up were pretty much in line with industry standards, and few of the X Factor competitors were likely to lose much sleep at a clause giving Sony – and by extension Cowell – final say on song releases. After all, X Factor competitors tend to be singers rather than musicians or songwriters. Their aim is to achieve fame and make some money rather than make their own music. A major part of X Factor's appeal is that winners are placed in the hands of expert managers, songwriters and producers who will mould them into hit-making shape and steer them to the top of the charts. X Factor is not a forum for songwriters or indie bands to promote their unique vision to the world.

But what the leaked contract did reveal was that Cowell, Syco and Sony ran a tight ship. If contestants benefitted from the show by touring the country and playing to packed houses, then Cowell and his colleagues would benefit from their success. If a runner-up had greater hit potential than the ultimate winner, then Cowell could be first in the queue with a record deal offer. And with a management partner on hand in the shape of Modest!, Cowell could be sure that *X Factor* winners would be in the hands of a company he knew and trusted. Or to put it another way, all the bases were covered.

KNOW WHEN TO BE FLEXIBLE

Despite these seemingly tight contracts, Cowell has also indicated that in certain circumstances he is prepared to waive his contractual rights. The scenario of a manager, record label boss or agent ruthlessly exploiting an artist who has failed to read the contractual small print is a familiar one in novels, screenplays and press exposes. But the truth is that holding a performer to a contract is likely to be counterproductive unless the individual in question is able and willing to make the relationship work.

The issue was raised during the ascent of Susan Boyle, the undoubted star of the 2009 season of *Britain's Got Talent*. Having shot to fame on the back of a tremendous singing voice, Boyle began to show signs that she was buckling under the strain of dealing with the media and appearing on a hugely competitive show. Some questioned whether she should be taken off the show for the sake of her own mental health.

While still competing on *Got Talent*, Boyle had already signed a record deal with Syco and there was clearly big money to be made from a singer who was establishing a global reputation and following. But speaking on GMTV, Cowell revealed that he had been prepared to cancel the contract if either she or her family felt that the pressures of show business had become too much. 'I said to her family, I'll rip the contract up, you can have the contract back', he said. 'No one's going to force her into the recording studio – I'll do whatever Susan wants … And we've done what she wants us to do.'[5]

Few people know the full details of that conversation and, indeed, how willingly he would have given up the option of an artist who had platinum disc potential. In the event, Boyle proved more resilient that some had feared, returning to the stage and recording a best-selling debut album for Cowell's label after a spell in the Priory rehabilitation clinic. However, what Cowell had shown was that he is aware of the moral and ethical responsibilities of steering potentially vulnerable people from obscurity to money-making stardom. An artist who, for whatever reason, is unable to cope with the limelight is a liability rather than an asset. Clearly, flexibility on a contract of that nature is simply good business sense.

GET THE BEST FROM YOUR ASSETS

Perhaps the biggest annual challenge facing Simon Cowell is the transformation of the *X Factor* winner into a hit recording artist. On the face of it, he can't lose. The public elects a winner and unless something completely unexpected happens, the momentum of the competition carries the anointed one to the top of the charts over the Christmas period. In the UK, *X Factor* works to a clearly defined calendar. The show ends just a few weeks before Christmas and by the time the winner has been voted in by the public, the three contestants who survive to the series finale have recorded a song that can be released immediately.

That's the easy part. The bigger challenge is to take the winning artist away and record a debut album for release long after that particular series has been forgotten by the viewer.

And, of course, Cowell has no real choice over who he works with. Critics tend to depict him as a pop Machiavelli who rules *X Factor* (and indeed *American Idol* and *Britain's Got Talent*) with a rod of iron, using his influence to dictate the course of events and the ultimate choice of winner. However, at the end of the day the winner is chosen by the public and we can only assume that Cowell doesn't always get the winner he would choose in an ideal world.

That was certainly true when he made his judging debut on *Pop Idol*. In the first series of that show he seemed to favour Gareth Gates over the eventual winner Will Young. Cowell probably shot himself in the foot on that occasion. Such was his advocacy of Gates that he didn't feel he could work with the victorious Young. There were no casualties. Young was signed by Sony BMG anyway and went on to forge a stellar career without Cowell's help. Meanwhile Gates was signed by Cowell and was also highly successful. Perhaps the only modest loser was Cowell himself as he had to make do with just one rather than two successful acts on his own portfolio.

But even if you can't always get who you want, Cowell has shown that if the talent is there he can do great things with his winning acts. Leona Lewis is a case in point. Just 22 when she won *X Factor*, she was clearly a cut above the vast bulk of competitors who have appeared in the show over the years. Although she was young and relatively inexperienced, she had the voice and presence to stand alongside the likes of Whitney Houston in the soul/pop diva pantheon. Her talent meant that she had potential to sell shiploads of CDs, not just in the UK but around the world. To his credit, Cowell recognized this from the off and did everything he could to ensure she fulfilled her potential.

His strategy was instructive. Rather than attempting to do every-thing in-house, Cowell partnered with Clive Davis, a legendary US music producer, A&R man and record industry executive. Now in his 80s, Davis was president of Columbia Records in the late 1960s and early 1970s before moving to the Arista label where a young Whitney Houston was among his signings. Today he is Chief Creative Officer at Sony BMG where he also presides over his own J (Jive) Records label. It is to J Records that Leona Lewis is signed.

Under the double-headed mentoring of Davis and Cowell, Lewis was not only given the chance to work with some of the world's leading producers and song-writers in the pop-soul field, she was also afforded the luxury of taking some degree of control over the development of her music.

Lewis was given the time and studio expertise to make an album that would not simply sell, it would establish her as a diva to be reckoned with.

'I've been treated as my own person,' she says in a profile posted on the RCA Records website. 'I've not been given a for-mula to follow. I had the time to find my feet and co-write a lot of material. I've learned a lot and Simon and Clive really listen to me.'[6]

Indeed, Lewis' account of her first year working for Syco and J Records suggests that when Cowell is in the presence of someone he recognizes has talent, he is prepared to cut the artist some slack rather than trying to control every aspect of career development and musical output.

The reward for Lewis, Cowell and David was a hugely successful debut album that managed the hitherto unheard of achievement of going straight into the Billboard album charts at Number One. The first single from the album – Bleeding Love – also made the number one spot.

All of this demonstrates that Cowell isn't always thinking of the fast buck. After the quick win of the post-*X Factor* Christmas single, Lewis was given the time and studio expertise to make an album that would not simply sell, it would establish her as a diva to be reckoned with. When it was released, the album boasted credible songs and heavyweight production. It was a marker to show that Lewis would be in the music business for the long term.

Cowell's treatment of artists and bands largely depends on his assessment of their appeal to the public. Compare and contrast Lewis's debut album with that of Robson and Jerome. The former contained contemporary songwriting tailored for the artist. The latter was a collection of karaoke favourites. The difference was, of course, that Robson and Jerome were actors with a retro appeal and decent if unspectacular voices. Their albums were tailored to the audience that Cowell had identified. In doing so he ensured that both he and the two actors received the maximum payout. Lewis had a world class voice that would bear comparison with some of the best singers in the world. She had potential to reach far beyond the Saturday night TV audience and she was treated accordingly.

KNOW WHEN TO LET GO

Cowell has made is clear that artists signed to Syco – and we can assume that this particularly applies to those brought on board via a TV series – have to earn their keep. When a winner bounces off the *X Factor* stage, the company will certainly honour its obligation to record and release records on behalf of the artist but no one – least of all Cowell – is promising a long-term future.

'We can't guarantee that they will be an international star,' he told the *Sun* newspaper. 'There is a 50/50 chance that they are going to make it. Sometimes it doesn't work.'[7]

And a management partner on hand in the shape of Modest!, Cowell could be sure that *X Factor* winners would be managed by a company he knew and trusted.

As Cowell acknowledged, the singer who is popular with a Saturday night TV audience may only have limited appeal as a recording artist once they've left the show. '… it's out of our hands – it comes down to the public whether or not they like them after the show.'

And when an act comes off the boil, fails to make a real connection with record buyers, or displays inappropriate independence of mind, the chances are that he or she will be leaving the Syco stable and returning to the real world relatively quickly. The casualties to date include *X Factor* winners Steve Brookstein and Leon Jackson, both of whom racked up just one album each for the label following their victories.

Brookstein's experience, as described during an interview with *The Times* indicates that artistic freedom is not something that is generally encouraged within the Cowell empire. He managed 12 weeks with the label, despite racking up a British number one with Phil Collins' 'Against All Odds'. As a popular winner, he should have been in line for a run of hits but wasn't happy with the material chosen for him or the image he was required to present to the world:

'Simon kept saying, "I know what I'm doing," by which he meant, "I know what sells." But it sounded like karaoke to me … I was offered £12,500 to go away quietly, and when I didn't take it, life got very difficult.'[8]

Cowell might question that version of events, but the fact remains that, with a few exceptions, the singers who join Syco should expect the professionals who run the company to call the shots. Only the very, very talented can expect to wrest a degree of control over image and musical direction.

Cowell's apparent unwillingness to work with artists such as Steve Brookstein, who have a mind of their own, is often used by critics as a rod to beat him. It is evidence that he is nothing more than a pop Svengali who exploits his artists and then discards them.

The majority of contestants are prepared to put their careers in his hands to achieve the fame and fortune that would probably otherwise elude them.

There's truth in that but it's a critique that misses two important points. Firstly Cowell is transparently in it for the money. His background is as a maker of hits and he trusts his own judgment – and that of his professional associates – when it comes to selecting songs and marketing records. That confidence is underpinned by his own track record. He is unlikely to listen to those who don't have a track record in the music industry, unless they can make a very good case for doing it their way rather than his.

Secondly, those who sign to his label do so with their eyes open. Just as Cowell is looking for fresh blood through which to maintain his hold on the TV and record buying audience, the majority of contestants are prepared to put their careers in his hands to achieve the fame and fortune that would probably otherwise elude them.

For some, the label can be a launch pad to different, if not greater things. For instance, Rhydian Roberts, who joined the label as *X Factor* runner-up in 2007, quit in 2010 to pursue a career as a classical singer rather than a pop-crossover act. He was, however, generous in his praise of the Cowell operation, even at the point of departure. 'In creative terms, [Syco] don't have the right approach or experience when it comes to classical music … *The X Factor* and Simon Cowell were definitely a good launch pad for me. … And I'll always be grateful to the three-and-a-half million people who voted for me.'[9]

For those who fall by the wayside, the outcome can be messy. Steve Brookstein's interview with *The Times* indicates that he is still scarred by his experience of tasting fame and having it taken away again. Even the pleasure of playing small gigs in pubs is denied to him as he fears being sniffed out by tabloid journalists 'taking the piss.'

But at the end of the day, Cowell is a leopard who is in no hurry to change his spots. The view that he – or at least the label – knows best has served him well and he is unlikely to abandon that philosophy. As a record company boss, it's in Cowell's interests to get as much out of those assets as possible, which means managing and nurturing the talent to maximize sales potential.

CHASE WHEN NECESSARY

Which is not to say that Cowell doesn't take time to woo those that he would like to work with him. In a previous chapter, we touched on his eagerness to sign Robson Green and Jerome Flynn, two actors who achieved fame through the *Soldier Soldier* TV series in the 1990s.

Enthused by the popularity of their on-screen performance of 'Unchained Melody', Cowell tried for months to sign the pair and received rebuttal after rebuttal for his pains. Nevertheless, he continued to pursue them, even (according to legend, so perhaps best taken with a sizeable pinch of salt) approaching Green's mother in a bid to gain leverage. Eventually the actors gave in. From then, though, it was strictly a record-company-knows-best situation, with Cowell playing a major role in selecting songs for the duo's two albums.

It's easy to depict the relationship between Cowell and those on his label as a kind of deal with the devil – in return for an undertaking that you will do what Simon says, you will be given untold riches. The fact that it's a deal that people are queuing up to make is testimony to his reputation as a man who knows what sells, knows how to sell it and keeps his hands firmly on the steering wheel.

MANAGE THE TALENT

Cowell is a star in his own right but his reputation as music mogul depends on his ability to successfully exploit the talent signed to Syco records.

- **Keep the contracts tight.** As a leaked contract relating to *X Factor* reveals, Cowell and Sony keep contestants on the show under a tight rein. Under the terms of the agreement, winners must sign to Syco and the company also has first option on the runners-up. There has been some controversy over the £150,000 advance paid to *X Factor* winners and the promise of a £1m deal made on the show. However, as Sony has pointed out, the overall value of the deal could be £1m or more.

  Tight contracts are hugely important when parties enter into complex business arrangements as they ensure that everyone is clear on their rights and obligations, and legally bound by the terms.
- **Know when to be flexible.** Whatever the line of business, it may not always make sense to enforce contractual agreements if sticking by the letter of the document is going to be counterproductive for those involved. Cowell has indicated a willingness to relax his contractual grip on artists who might be unsuited to the pressures of public life.
- **Get the best from your assets.** As Cowell has demonstrated with Leona Lewis, when faced with a singer of world class potential, Cowell is prepared to allow his signings time to develop and a degree of artistic control. In the case of Lewis, Cowell has worked in partnership with

music industry veteran Clive Davis. Together, the two men put Lewis in the hands of top producers, songwriters and musicians. The result was an album that established her as a genuine soul diva. Like all good businessmen Cowell is prepared to invest in his assets.

- **Know when to let go.** Syco records is not a permanent home. Those whose careers decline or who clash with Cowell are often dropped. It's a matter of focusing resources on those who will deliver sales.

- **Chase when necessary.** As his pursuit of Robson and Jerome illustrates, Cowell is prepared to go to enormous lengths to woo and sign acts that he believes have sales potential. Persistence is an important element in his business success.

9

LEARN TO ROLL WITH THE PUNCHES

'Failure is good as long as it doesn't become a habit.'[1]

– Michael Eisner, Disney Corporation

L et's think role reversal for a moment. In a parallel universe, Simon Cowell is pitching for investment on the TV show *Dragons' Den*. He is, as ever, brimming with confidence as he explains how his company, Syco, will produce peak time TV shows designed to discover bankable talent that can be sold to the public via the same company's record label. The Dragons – all entrepreneurs with real money to invest – scent a major business opportunity and they want to know more about the man behind the concept. The plan is incredibly ambitious so they're keen to discover whether Cowell has the experience and track record to really deliver what he's promising.

And under the glare of the TV lights Cowell fills them in. Two decades working as an A&R man. A solid run of hit records in the 1990s. Experience of running his own labels and working within major corporations. It all looks good, but in the middle of it all there's something very worrying. The man who is promising to take the world by storm suffered an enormous setback in the middle of his career. Fanfare Records, the company he was instrumental in building, ceased trading when it went bankrupt. Meanwhile, Cowell had a mountain of personal debts to pay.

The Dragons pause for thought. All entrepreneurs know that businesses fail. They also know the collapse of one venture won't necessarily mean that those behind the company won't succeed next time round. Nevertheless, they look at Cowell – now approaching middle age – and wonder whether they should back him. Looking him up and down, the Dragons launch into a series of questions. Why did the business go under? How did you get back on your feet? What did you learn?

It's a make or break moment. Will Cowell give a good account of himself or will he buckle under the questions?

Back in the real world, Cowell has never had to face the hard-nosed investors who populate the *Dragons' Den* but he certainly has had to pick himself up and dust himself down in the wake of a company failure. Fanfare Records closed because of problems with the parent company but its demise represented a major personal and professional setback for Cowell. Arguably, it was also a watershed in his career. With Fanfare dead, he returned to work as an A&R consultant for BMG records and began the ascent from little-known label boss with a modestly successful track record to his current position of high profile media mogul. We don't know if Cowell's career would have been any more or less successful had Fanfare survived, but what we can say is that he rolled with the punches of business failure and carried on fighting.

The collapse of Fanfare Records is by no means the only black spot on the Cowell CV. Truth to tell, he hasn't always made it easy for himself. As we know, he was not a fan of school, E&S Records did not serve up any real success when he was at the helm and, more recently, there was a real possibility that his flagship TV project *X Factor* would be choked at birth by a lawsuit from partner and rival Simon Fuller.

None of above setbacks could be described as trivial, but Cowell has consistently managed to stay positive in difficult times and overcome adversity.

LEARN FROM YOUR PARENTS

One of the attributes that tends to separate entrepreneurs and corporate high flyers from the rest of the population is a sense of their ability to turn their ideas into reality. Most of us have business ideas from time to time and some of them might even be great ideas. However, unless we take the necessary steps to transform a basic concept into a living, breathing, wealth-generating business then the idea will be of little use or value.

Entrepreneurs act. They set objectives, formulate strategies, raise cash and cold call customers. Those who have been successful in business tend to make reassuring noises about the process of launching a business or a new venture within a larger organization. Phrases such as 'it's not rocket science' or 'anyone can do it' tend to be bandied about a lot along with the basic mantra that success is grounded in hard work and dedication.

We don't know if Cowell's career would have been any more or less successful had Fanfare survived, but what we can say is that he rolled with the punches of business failure.

That's largely true, but self-confidence plays an important role too. Entrepreneurs typically have a can-do approach to life. Once they come up with an idea, the working assumption is that they have the ability to move it forward and ultimately create a successful business. Those with less self belief are more likely to think in terms of the obstacles rather than the opportunities. 'I could do this, but there are just too many problems to overcome.'

Confidence can be a fragile thing and Cowell's relatively low level of attainment at school might well have delivered a killer blow to his self-esteem and ego, particularly as he enjoyed a privileged education at not one but two private institutions. In fact, accounts of Cowell's teenage years suggest that he left school brimming with ambition. Underpinning that ambition was the confidence and self belief that often comes from growing up in a nurturing, happy and financially successful family, coupled with a key message, imparted by his parents, that success and hard work are closely related.

The work ethic was imbued from an early age. For instance, speaking to Lynn Barber – the *Observer* newspaper's queen of the celebrity interview – Cowell described an adolescence that combined comfort of life in a well-off family with regular injections of financial reality. Or, to be more precise, reminders that he would one day have to work, and work hard, for a living. For instance, the parental rules of the road stated that Cowell would live rent free and, while holidays would be paid for, Cowell would have to find work and earn his own spending money. 'I loved having my own money. In school holidays I would always apply for jobs … I was always happier working than just mucking around,'[2] he said.

School bored him and he apparently had few doubts that hard work and industry would enable him to transcend his poor level of academic achievement. The example of his parents may have played a role here too. Eric Cowell had been very successful in the property business and while there are plenty of people in real estate with qualifications to burn, it's not an industry where certificates are required or seen as evidence of worth.

And in his chosen business – the music industry – Cowell entered a similar meritocracy. You don't need an O level to spot talent and market hit records. What you need is a sense of what will sell and plenty of drive. Cowell had both in abundance, but again it was his parents who played a major role in helping him find his niche. As we've seen in earlier chapters, Eric Cowell used his influence to get his son a position at EMI. Without that start in life, his career path might have been very different.

ACKNOWLEDGE FAILURE

The abrupt closure of Fanfare Records was a much bigger blow to Cowell than his failure to shine academically. The shutting down of the company was potentially a killer blow to a career that was really just starting. As we know, Cowell's time at Fanfare saw him scoring his first singles chart bullseye with Sinitta's 'So Macho'. More hits followed – many in association with Stock Aitkin and Waterman – and Cowell could reasonably expect his career to flourish.

Instead the company closed, and although Cowell was not personally bankrupt, he was without a means to earn money. The trappings of success – his home, his Porsche – were taken away from him and he was weighed down by personal debt that had to be repaid. Famously, he was forced to abandon his independence and return to his parents' house where he would live for the next five years.

Events of this nature effect individuals on a number of levels. First and foremost, watching a business that you own or manage close down is a major psychological blow. Everything you've worked for disappears overnight, employees and colleagues lose their jobs and everyone's plans for future projects come to a sudden halt.

There is often a sense of personal culpability. Some business failures are down to internal problems – poor investment, bad cash flow management, low sales, to name but three – while others are caused by factors outside the control of management. For instance, the market may change or a major customer goes bust, leaving the business with a shortfall in income. But whatever the reason, most owners and senior management feel some sense of responsibility. Cowell admitted as much when he spoke about the incident to the *Independent*. Recalling his time running the label he described how he began to believe his own hype while working alongside employees who tended to simply agree with that he had to say. The closure of Fanfare ultimately prompted him to look hard at his own role in its demise. '… you start blaming the world, then you realize that, actually, it's you that got yourself into this situation.'[3]

You don't need an O level to spot talent and market hit records. What you need is a sense of what will sell and plenty of drive.

Then there is the financial impact. In an ideal world, those who run companies should be insulated from the impact of a failed business. For instance, in the case of limited companies, it is the business itself that is responsible for any debts rather than the directors and owners. In theory that means that while the company may go bust, the individuals who own it shouldn't be fending off creditors seeking to relieve them of their personal wealth. In the real world, the distinction between corporate and personal liability is often much more fuzzy. By law a director may not be responsible for a company's debts but, in practice, he or she may have been required to offer personal security to gain access to finance. The upshot is that a great many directors are pursued by creditors and possibly face the threat of personal insolvency when their companies go under. In the case of Fanfare the problems lay with the parent company but by Cowell's own account, he was certainly left high and dry with debts he found difficult to pay.

RESUME THE CLIMB

Less easy to quantify is the impact on a future career. It's often said that while US entrepreneurs regard business failure as a fact of life, their UK counterparts see it as a stigma. That attitude is slowly changing and, in recent years, the UK government has strived to create a bankruptcy regime that makes it easier for business people to get back on their feet and start again. Nevertheless, a certain stigma remains and a businessman who picks himself up and attempts to start again may well find it difficult to raise finance or even find a job.

But Cowell not only survived the collapse of Fanfare, he flourished. He returned to the music business and became more successful than ever.

It's often said that while US entrepreneurs regard business failure as a fact of life, their British counterparts see it as a stigma.

He was, perhaps, luckier than most. He could, once again, fall back on the good will and support offered by his parents. Many people would find it uncomfortable to return to the family home after living an independent lifestyle for many years, but Cowell had a good relationship with his mother and father and having a safe and secure base allowed him to pick up the pieces and get on with his life.

Cowell's route back to success was a re-entry to the corporate world. Rather than attempt to start another label – either on his own or in partnership with others – he took a job as an A&R consultant at BMG records.

With the 20/20 vision of hindsight, it was a smart move. Fanfare had given Cowell a vehicle in which he could learn about the music business first hand and hone his skills both as an A&R man – working with artists and selecting songs – and a label boss.

On the face of it, the failure of Fanfare meant that he'd lost everything, but he still had his hard-won industry knowledge and his instinct for a hit. Within a well-funded organization such as BMG, he had an opportunity to build on his track record. It was an opportunity that he grasped with both hands.

If anything, he turned up the heat. With Fanfare, Cowell had certainly focused on signing mainstream pop acts with hit potential but the label was, in many respects, quite conventional in terms of its portfolio. The likes of Sinitta, Gloria Gaynor and Curiosity Killed the Cat were singers and bands in the old-fashioned sense of the word, signed to the label on the strength of their looks, singing ability and appeal to a young, dance-oriented audience.

But as we've seen in earlier chapters, Cowell's career at BMG hit a different stride. He was still signing pop talent – Westlife being a case in point – but there was a new hunger for hits, with Cowell prepared to consider just about any project that would yield a return. Thus, we had records based on kid's TV characters (Power Rangers, Zig and Zag) and stars of the World Wrestling Foundation. And, for the mums and dads, we had the actors Robson and Jerome singing karaoke classics.

None of this did any good at all for Cowell's standing as an A&R man with music in his blood, but it sealed his reputation as an industry player who could be trusted to bring home the bacon. S Records – founded by Cowell within BMG in 2000 – became a very profitable unit. The man himself was back on top. His renaissance certainly wasn't a given – it was based on determination, hard work and focus on revenue-generating projects.

After a decade spent working for independent labels, Cowell could have been forgiven for deciding the music industry wasn't for him. Instead, he built on what he'd learned at EMI, E&S and Fanfare and took his own career to a higher level.

HAVE YOUR DAY OUT OF COURT

Since then it seems that Cowell has done nothing but track upwards on an increasingly steep trajectory. Working for (and with) BMG and subsequently Sony, he has left the financial problems of Fanfare far behind and established himself as the richest man on TV.

But there was one more potential obstacle that Cowell would have to overcome before donning the mantle of internationally renowned media mogul. That obstacle took the shape of television and music industry partner Simon Fuller.

Cowell and Fuller were at the centre of the team that conceived the 'find a star' reality show *Pop Idol*. First sold to ITV, the concept was soon afterwards successfully pitched as *American Idol* to Fox Network in the US. It was *Idol* that made Cowell's name, establishing him as the Mr Nasty that everyone loved to hate.

As the undisputed star of the show, Cowell gained a huge amount of traction in the media industry. So much so that when he came up with his own idea for a follow-up in the shape of *X Factor*, ITV jettisoned *Idol* in favour of the Cowell creation.

This was bound to put a huge amount of strain on the Cowell/Fuller partnership. Fuller's 19 Entertainment owned the *Idol* franchise. When *X Factor* first appeared on British screens, *American Idol* was still running in the US, with Cowell earning good money as the kingpin of the judging panel. The upshot was that Cowell was continuing to profit from *Idol* having launched a rival series in the UK. Perhaps, not surprisingly, Fuller took exception to this turn of events and called in his lawyers.

The resulting legal action accused Cowell, his two companies Syco and Simco, and production partner Fremantle Media of breaching copyright, with the allegation partly based on perceived similarities between *Pop Idol* and *X Factor*.

It threatened to be a landmark ruling that would define the extent to which TV formats could be protected. This was something of a grey area. *X Factor* certainly had a lot in common with *Idol*: auditions, a record deal for the winner, a judging panel, and a process through which a potential pop star would be selected in a competitive process stretched over the weeks of a series. In fact, Fuller named more than 20 similarities between the two shows.

For their part, Cowell's camp pointed to the differences between the shows, including features not seen on *Idol*. These included a boot camp where more than a hundred hopefuls selected from the open audition stage would be coached and put through their paces. And when the finalists for the knockout stage were selected, Cowell had introduced a system into which the contestants would be put into groups, with each of these mentored by a judge. Robust in his defence of the *X Factor* format he described Fuller's copyright action as 'totally and utterly ridiculous.'[4]

Cowell's career at BMG hit a different stride. He was still signing pop talent ... but there was a new hunger for hits.

Cowell's PR advisor Max Clifford also waded into the argument. Quoted by the BBC, Clifford pointed out that many television programmes bear a superficial similarity to each other, implying that a successful outcome for the Fuller camp could throw the industry into chaos. 'Does this mean that Granada could sue the BBC for creating *EastEnders* because it made *Coronation Street* first?'[5]

Fremantle Media were also quick to defend their position, 'We deny the allegations … [and] defend any action vigorously and we hope to resolve the matter amicably. *The X Factor* is a different format to *Pop Idol*.'[6]

The Cowell camp certainly had a point. *Idol* was in itself a variation on a theme already seen on TV in the series *Popstars* – indeed it even shared a producer in the shape of Nigel Lythgoe. And, as Clifford went on to point out, the producers of *Popstars* had unsuccessfully tried to sue the *Idol* production team.

So the courts had a thorny problem on their hands, namely to establish some ground rules on the degree to which one television show can resemble another without breaching copyright. It was a case that would be watched anxiously by the industry.

Fuller's case went beyond alleged similarities. As his lawsuit made clear he was also concerned about an alleged breach of contract, claiming a number of the *X Factor*'s production team also worked on *Pop Idol* where they signed contracts that restricted them from working on rival shows.

Things could have got very messy but the case was ultimately settled out of court. According to the *Independent* newspaper[7] this was partly at the behest of the Fox Network. There was a certainly a lot at stake for Fox. *American Idol* – hugely successful in the US – was renegotiating its contract with the network and Fox was keen to keep Cowell on board as a judge. The fear that a lawsuit in London would result in Cowell jumping from the *American Idol* ship was very real, with financial implications for all parties, including Cowell and Fuller.

Faced with the prospect that *American Idol* might lose its golden goose, a deal was done. The details of the deal were not revealed, but we do know that Cowell stayed with *American Idol* until 2010, while honouring an obligation not to take *X Factor* to the States for an agreed period. 'I don't think anyone was unhappy with what they got out of it'[8] Cowell told the *Independent*.

It wasn't the only *Idol*/Cowell related case to be settled out of court. In 2004, Ronagold – a company set up by Cowell and BMG records to record and market *Pop Idol* winners – sued Fuller's 19 Entertainment, alleging that the latter was seeking to divert victorious contestants to different labels. That dispute was also settled out of court.

So, in the end, enlightened self-interest won the day. Media reports tend to play up the huge rivalry between Cowell and Fuller – and the competitive edge that both men share was certainly on display during the *Idol*/*X Factor* dispute. Ultimately though, they opted to put business first.

Over a career spanning three decades, it would be surprising if Cowell hadn't had his share of peaks and troughs, and arguably he's had fewer real disasters than many ambitious businessmen. But the fact remains that in his early career he persevered past the non performance of E&S and bounced back in the wake of Fanfare's demise. In both cases, he could simply have thrown in his hand and tried another industry. Later, he was robust enough to stand up to a court action by a former partner. Thanks to a mix of self-confidence, strength of purpose and – in the case of the court action – a willingness to settle, he kept his career moving forward.

LEARN TO ROLL WITH THE PUNCHES

Simon Cowell's career has been marked by setbacks, ranging from poor academic attainment to high-profile lawsuits and a failed company. He has not only survived these setbacks but thrived, becoming ever more successful.

- **Learn from your parents.** Cowell came from a loving home and despite some wayward behaviour in his teens and a poor academic record, they continued to provide help and support. His father engineered his first real job – at EMI Records – but perhaps more importantly, both his mother and father continued to stress the importance of hard work. Cowell was encouraged to earn money as a child and as he set out on his record industry career he knew that in order to succeed he would have to work hard.
- **Acknowledge failure.** When Fanfare Records collapsed, Cowell could have taken his leave of the music industry. After ten years, he was back to square one. But Cowell had by now established a genuine track record in finding artists and songs with hit potential. Shortly after Fanfare's demise he put those skills to work at BMG. A determination to bounce back after failure is an essential trait for the entrepreneur. Not every project will succeed and some will fail badly. The important thing is to learn from the failure rather than let it drag you down.
- **Resume the climb.** Cowell not only survived, he turned up the heat. During his time as a BMG executive he had more hits than ever and established a reputation for getting novelty records into the charts. Despite earlier set-

backs Cowell had the confidence to move his career forward and do things his own way.

- **Have your day out of court.** The success of *X Factor* was threatened by a lawsuit from *Pop Idol* rights owner and creator Simon Fuller. The court action could have had severe financial implications for both men and the TV networks who were paying them good money to turn out high rating shows. Ultimately they settled out of court. When companies clash on legal issues, a negotiated settlement is often better than a taking the risk of an all-or-nothing defeat or victory.

10

GET YOUR NAME ON THE TITLE

'It should be everyone's birthright to get the chance to fulfil their dream. Yes, for some it's being a pop star. But for many more hard-working Brits, it's something far less flash – it's starting your own business.'[1]

– Simon Cowell

As he continues to grow his global television and music interests, Simon Cowell is in an enviable position. He's rich. He has a close and mutually beneficial commercial relationship with Sony. And, above all, he's in control of his own destiny to a degree that most people in or outside the music and entertainment industries can only dream of.

But Cowell's autonomy has been hard won. As we've seen, his early attempts to work independently of the big guns of the record industry ended in failure. E&S produced no hits when Cowell was with the company and financial difficulties stopped Fanfare in its tracks.

Since then Cowell has adopted a different strategy. Rather than working independently of the music industry, he built his businesses in partnership with a corporate. First with BMG and now (following a takeover) with Sony, while remaining a high-profile leader rather than a cog in the bigger machine. It's been a neat trick.

Cowell's route to autonomy – or semi-autonomy – within a larger corporate structure has been long and winding. Following the closure of his Fanfare record label in the late 1980s, he was rescued by BMG who offered him a job as an A&R consultant. It was a position that allowed him to build a power base within the company as his ability to find talent and mastermind hit records became apparent.

However, it wasn't until 2000 that he and his company agreed to the creation of S Records as a 50/50 joint venture. Later, with the launch of *X Factor* on the near horizon, he moved to establish a successor to S that would allow him to pursue his multi-media ambitions. Syco was born.

That company remains at the centre of his plans today, but in its relatively short lifespan its ownership structure has been subject to negotiation and renegotiation. In the early days, Cowell had a stake in the business. This was later sold to Sony and, while its founder remained in control, the entertainment giant assumed 100% ownership. This all changed in 2010. With the Cowell contract up for renewal, the partners repackaged Syco as a 50/50 joint venture. Today, Cowell is not only still in the driving seat, he once again owns a substantial piece of the action.

Like most other industries, the entertainment industry rewards success. A successful A&R man working with a roster of artists can reasonably expect a share of the profits when the hit records begin to mount up.

Like all joint ventures, the Syco arrangement represents an example of enlightened self-interest in action. From Sony's perspective, Cowell is one of a rare breed of golden geese laying golden eggs. Well, let's not forget we're in the hyped-up world of the record and entertainment industries here, so let's say that he's a fully-fledged platinum goose. And with Syco responsible for a significant percentage of Sony's UK profits, it made sense for the entertainment giant to give its star A&R performer what he wanted in terms of a 50% share in the business.

Meanwhile, Cowell continues to work with a company that has been a long-term partner and one with the resources that can help him put his ideas into practice. Meanwhile, his name remains firmly engraved above the door of Syco for the foreseeable future.

The upshot of all this is that Cowell is a living embodiment of the old maxim, you don't get rich on a salary. Like most other industries, the entertainment industry rewards success. A successful A&R man working with a roster of artists can reasonably expect a share of the profits when the hit records begin to mount up.

But one way or another, Cowell has probably managed to secure a bigger piece of the action than most. That's partly down to joint venture deals that ensure he gets his fair share of any money made, but in addition to that, the creation of 'Brand Simon' has of course secured him a multi-million pound income stream from TV appearances. As a 'name' within the industry, he is in a much better position to grow his business interests and his fortune than he was as an obscure backroom boy working in an airless office, known only to his colleagues and industry peers.

So let's take a closer look at the benefits that autonomy coupled with a high industry profile have brought to Cowell.

ESTABLISH THE FREEDOM TO DO WHAT YOU WANT

On a personal level, Cowell has arrived at a point in his career where he gets to make his own rules. Anyone who has spent any time at all working within a corporate structure – or even working for an entrepreneur in a start-up – knows that the working day runs along tracks set down by others higher up the organizational tree.

It's not something most of us get hung up about, of course. In taking a job and accepting the salary package we implicitly agree to fit in with the culture, management practices and strategies of the organization in question. We may think we could do it better but at the end of the day, we're mostly not in a position to make the changes we'd like to see.

Not surprisingly, Cowell is not someone who particularly relishes doing things according to the whims and dictates of others. As he told the *Observer*, money, success and the autonomy they bring have provided him with a means to step outside the strictures of corporate life and, effectively, make his own rules.

'I've always been petrified of working for a boss who I didn't like but who I was in fear of, because I wanted my salary',[2] he told Lynn Barber.

And if Cowell found the corporate conventions painful, many of his colleagues doubtless found his attitudes hard to take. In the same interview, he recalls sitting through a presentation at a conference and laughing during an executive's presentation. Needless to say, it wasn't at a point in the speech where mirth was expected, warranted or welcomed and Cowell was asked to leave the room.

It was a petty indignity but in Cowell's mind it was a textbook example of why it is better to run a company than work as an employee.

BECOME A TALENT MAGNET

Cowell's profile within the industry and, indeed, with the public at large, have enabled him to become a talent magnet – someone who is able to work with some of the best and most experienced people in the entertainment industry. Equally important there are plenty of would-be pop stars who would sacrifice limbs in order to have the *X Factor* magician guiding their careers.

All careers survive, thrive or perish on the back of working relationships. Sometimes those relationships are purely internal. You do a job, you do it well and that fact is recognized by those around you. That recognition creates a profile within the business – a profile that will help define the direction of your career.

Very often relationships stretch well beyond the four walls of a particular organization. For instance, a salesman will establish relationships with customers. Over time as they come to trust him, selling becomes easier. Some customers will see him as the face of the company and when he goes elsewhere, they follow.

Not surprisingly, Cowell is not someone who particularly relishes doing things according to the whims and dictates of others.

And then there are the relationships with business partners, the suppliers and advisors and other firms who help the company achieve its goals. Let's say a business wants to set up a joint venture with another company. The negotiations are going to be a lot easier if the key players within both organizations already know each other, either personally or by reputation.

For the truth is that if you're looking for people to work with – either within or outside your organization – it's much easier if you have a good reputation and a visible track record of success.

That's certainly been true for Cowell. By setting up ventures that are clearly defined and successful, Cowell has enhanced his profile within the industry. By talking directly to consumers via *Pop*

Idol and *X Factor* he has created a profile that extends beyond his peer group and into the wider world. People know who he is, what he does, why he does it and the results he achieves. That in turn makes it easier for him to strike deals and establish working relationships, as Cowell himself acknowledged in an interview with trade magazine *Music Week*: 'It's easier for me now because I think more talented people want to work with me now than they did five years ago … Me on my own, I'm useless. I'm just someone spouting off whatever is in my mind. With talented record producers, TV producers and executives, I'm good.'[3]

LEAD WITH VISION

When Cowell set up S Records as a joint venture with Sony BMG he announced that his intention was to create a label focused on pure pop. 'It will be exactly the same as I've always done and this is why I want to do it, because that way I can absolutely concentrate on this area',[3] he told *Music Week*.

It was a comment that highlighted one of the main advantages of running an independent company or a business unit with a high degree of autonomy. As the man or woman in charge of a clearly defined entity, you have the opportunity to pursue a vision and create a business that bears your imprimatur.

On the face of it, the move to set up S Records had financial implications for both parties – it was a 50/50 joint venture – but wouldn't necessarily represent a sea change in the way Cowell was perceived within the industry. He was, after all, already very much in the 'pure pop' arena and under the terms of the deal his existing portfolio of artists, including Westlife and Five, would migrate to the new label. So not much change there then.

Arguably though, the establishment of S Records marked another step in the creation of Cowell, albeit partially within the confines of the Sony BMG family. He wasn't simply an A&R man with a portfolio of artists, he was once again a label boss.

And a label boss with ambitions. The creation of S Records predated both *Pop Idol* and *X Factor* but Cowell and his label certainly went on to reap the rewards of an association with the former. Under the terms of his agreement with Simon Fuller, *Pop Idol* winners were obliged to record under Cowell and BMG's flag. As main man at S and as key player in the *Pop Idol* team he could see how a symbiotic relationship between a televised talent show and a record label could work. And he could also see the benefits of creating a company that handled all aspects of the TV/recording operation, from production to ownership of the rights.

Cowell's profile within the industry and, indeed, with the public at large, have enabled him to become a talent magnet.

So, in that regard, the establishment of Syco was a natural next step. Cowell's vision was to create an end-to-end operation that reflected the crucial role television was going to play in his talent recruitment, development and marketing strategies. And Syco was a platform from which he could articulate his vision.

Think of it this way. As we've seen in previous chapters, the process of bringing *X Factor* and *Britain's Got Talent* to the screen requires the input and expertise of a lot of different companies, each with their own areas of excellence. Would *X Factor* have got off the ground without Cowell to sell his vision to the various stakeholders? Clearly not. And would Cowell have been so successful in selling that vision if he hadn't shaped a company that was small, agile and geared towards multi media? Well perhaps, but it might have been a harder sell and Cowell may well have been working from a position of lesser influence than he enjoys today.

As it is, Syco not only owns the rights to *X Factor* and *Britain's Got Talent*, they are universally perceived as Cowell's babies. That is not to understate the contribution of the other partners. Without Sony, Fremantle and Thames Talkback, Syco's shows wouldn't be what they are today in terms of domestic popularity and global sales. But were you to ask the average man or woman on the legendary Clapham omnibus who is responsible for *X Factor* and *Got Talent*, no one is going to name an obscure Sony executive or a producer from Thames Talkback. The profits are shared, but it's Cowell who takes the credit. Through the vehicle of Syco he has nailed his vision and secured a global reputation.

That's not to say that Cowell and his team don't periodically have to sell their vision to parents and partners, but Cowell has undoubtedly been helped in that regard by the association with Sony/BMG that has endured over two decades. Early success in selling hit records off the back of television shows paved the way for the much more closely integrated relationship between *X Factor* and record sales. The success of *X Factor* then made shows such as *Got Talent* and *American Inventor* a more attractive option for the backers and production partners. Or to put it another way, those partners trust Cowell's vision.

OWN YOUR ASSETS

As we've seen, Cowell's long and fruitful relationship with BMG/Sony has taken a number of twists and turns in terms of his contractual and commercial relationship with the entertainment industry giant. He began life as an A&R consultant. With the creation of S Records, he took a 50% stake in a joint venture. When Syco was established he sold 100% ownership to Sony, only to negotiate himself a 50% stake in the company when his contract came up for renewal in 2010. A fairly torturous route by anyone's standards.

In terms of the day-to-day running of S and Syco, it probably didn't make a huge amount of difference where the ownership lay. Cowell was in charge, with his own team and roster of artists and interests, backed by the might of a global company.

He wasn't simply an A&R man with a portfolio of artists, he was once again a label boss.

But ownership does matter. The traditional route into employment is a salaried position with a fixed income every month. If you happen to be in a part of the business – say sales or A&R – where the bottom line of the company can be linked to your personal performance, then it makes sense for the employer to build in some sort of incentive scheme. This could take the form of a bonus based on the overall performance of the department or additional payments linked to your own work. Alternatively, the employer could issue share options giving everyone (or a selected few) a share of the upside when the company does well.

The aim of this is to align the interests of employees with those of the company and it's a great way of incentivizing staff. But none of these arrangements constitutes ownership. Employee share schemes probably come closest. In legalistic terms they represent a certain degree of ownership but most members of staff can expect to receive options amounting to only a tiny fraction of the overall value of the company so they are widely seen as financial benefits rather than conferring proprietary rights.

Holding a substantial stake in a business along with operational control is a very different matter. When Cowell set up S with a 50% holding, he became the joint owner of a successful business with valuable assets in terms of its artists, back catalogue and future potential. We can assume that he shared in the profits as an A&R consultant. But the ownership of S gave him other benefits as well.

First and foremost, he had something to sell. In the new era of a global talent marketplace, senior managers in both the public and private sector have been doing very nicely on the salary front, but the real potential to acquire wealth lies in holding a share in the business you work for. As the business grows, so does the value of the shareholding.

It's all paper wealth of course, tied up in the value of a business that can go down in value as well as up, but providing the company continues to increase its revenues and profits, a shareholding is an asset that will provide a healthy nest egg when the time comes to sell. Cowell sold his interests back to Sony BMG in 2003 in a deal that was reputedly worth somewhere in the region of £20–25m.

The Cowell model of integrating television and music production is beginning to look like an industry standard.

That begs a question. If ownership of the company is such a big deal, why give it up after a relatively short period of time? Only Cowell knows the answer to that, but we can assume that converting shares into the more liquid asset of cold hard cash played an important part in his thinking.

But in other respects, it was business as usual. Or, to be more precise, business as unusual. Cowell pressed ahead with plans for

Syco and seemed perfectly content to create his TV-music industry hybrid while handing over ownership of the venture to Sony.

That he was willing to do so indicated the depth of his relationship with the parent company. As Cowell told *Music Week*, BMG had given him a break following the demise of Fanfare Records and had been very supportive ever since. This support was repaid in the shape of Cowell's loyalty. 'I could have done a futures deal with any of the majors',[5] he said. He chose not to.

And within the Sony BMG structure, Cowell subsequently made himself pretty much essential. With its lean operation and big footprint covering TV and music, Syco rang up a huge percentage of the parent company's UK profits. Again, we can assume that Cowell's financial package reflected that success.

Fast forward to 2010 and it's all change again. If ownership gives you something to sell, then very visible success within an organization gives you a king-sized bargaining chip. Thus, when Cowell's contract with Sony came up for renewal, ownership was once again back on the table. Following a huge amount of speculation about Cowell's next move – perhaps in the direction of another label – it emerged that Cowell would once again have a major stake (50%) in his creation.

Underlying the wheeling and dealing is a simple message. Cowell's success, coupled with his visibility as a mover and shaker within BMG, has given him a huge amount of clout when it comes to negotiating contracts and striking deals on ownership. While we don't know if he gets exactly the deal that he wants, when he wants it, he seldom seems less than content with the outcome of his negotiations.

GET YOUR NAME ON THE TITLE

Over a thirty year career in the music and entertainment business, Simon Cowell has run a number of labels, but it is really over the last decade that he has come into his own as a highly visible record industry mogul. Since 2000 he has been in operational control of S Records and Syco, working as both an employee and an owner. His profile as the man running the show has been hugely important in terms of moving his career forward.

- **Establish the freedom to do what you want.** Cowell has never liked conforming to the culture of parent companies. As boss of S Records and Syco he has created his own culture. Like many businessmen working in a corporate environment he has discovered that success gives you freedom to do things your own way.
- **Become a talent magnet.** By becoming well known within the record and television industries, Cowell has become a talent magnet. People want to work with him. It's not simply that fresh-faced hopefuls entering the *X Factor* auditions see Cowell as their ticket to a better life. Success has meant he can work with influential people in both the television and music industries. Reputation is important regardless of industry. Well regarded people find it easier to recruit colleagues to projects and set up partnerships.
- **Lead with vision.** Cowell's vision of using TV to market music has resulted in a complex web of relationships between the production partners. He works closely with Sony, Fremantle and Talkback Thames, but it is his vision that has made the television shows and subsequent record releases so successful. Running a company has enabled

him to impart and control that vision. The ability to bring others in behind your vision is a mark of leadership.

- **Own your assets.** Part ownership of S Records and (latterly) Syco gives Cowell real assets that will grow in value as the business becomes more successful. Few of us can look forward to getting rich on a salary. Ownership of shares in a company or a stake in a joint venture provides a means to benefit from the success of the venture while sharing the risks with other stakeholders.

HOW TO DO BUSINESS
THE SIMON COWELL WAY

In some respects, Simon Cowell is a paradoxical figure. Known as a maverick, he is nonetheless a team player who works well with a wide range of partners, including Sony BMG. Seen as a consummate businessman with an independent and entrepreneurial streak, he has now worked with BMG and parent company Sony for the best part of two decades. Indeed, he has frequently declared his loyalty to the organization.

And yet, from within a corporate framework, he has emerged not only as a hugely successful record and television mogul but as a high-profile innovator who has changed the face of television and music marketing while getting very rich in the process.

This is how he's done it.

1   KNOW YOUR INDUSTRY

Simon Cowell has thirty years experience in the record and entertainment industries. Starting at the bottom as post boy for EMI records, he went on to become an A&R man for the company before leaving to start his own label with a colleague. As a label boss he learned from others, notched up hit records and tasted disaster when Fanfare Records closed. These early experiences have provided him with valuable lessons for his later career.

- Find a niche
- Get your foot in the door
- Take a gamble
- Be prepared to fight your space
- Learn from the best

2   KNOW YOUR AUDIENCE

Simon Cowell has a single goal – to sell enough CDs and down-loads to have hit records and make money for himself, his team and his employers. He is not hugely interested in critical acclaim. The success of a record released by the Cowell stable is judged by one thing only – whether or not it's a hit. A great record that nonetheless fails to make it to the higher reaches of the charts is a failure. Pure and simple. He has achieved his sales goals by learn-ing as much as possible about his audience.

- Know who you are selling to
- Follow the money
- Give your audience what they want
- Involve the market

3   HARNESS THE POWER OF THE CROWD

Over the last decade, Cowell's biggest successes have been secured through the participation of TV audiences around the world. Rather than sourcing artists by conventional means, he has used TV talent shows to find bankable stars. In other words, he has used the wis-dom of the crowd. It's a strategy that's paid huge dividends.

- Make the public work for you
- Incentivize the audience
- Act as ringmaster
- Keep the formula fresh
- Package the product
- Stay true to the business model
- Stay in control

4   THINK BIG, THINK LATERAL

Cowell's latter-day business model – using TV talent shows to source artists who are then signed to his record label – is both elegantly simply and bordering on pure genius. But if the concept is simple, making it work is a highly complex operation involving a diverse array of talented people.

- Get the structure right
- Hire the right people
- Bring partners on board
- Use all media outlets

5   DEVELOP INTERNATIONAL FORMATS

Selling the formats of successful Syco-owned shows is the key to Cowell's business strategy. You can see versions of *X Factor* in 40 countries around the world while shows based on the *Got Talent* format are shown in more than 30 territories. By selling formats, Cowell has become an international television industry player and he plans to expand his empire even further. Meanwhile *X Factor* is launching on US TV.

- Seize the market opportunities
- Exploit your profile
- Go global
- Think local when you act global
- Sell the original product
- Look to the future

6 WORK WITH PARTNERS

Throughout his career, working with partners has played an important part in Cowell's success. He may come across as his own man but he can collaborate effectively with a wide range of third parties.

- Divide the spoils
- Put business first
- Cast your net wider

7 TELL IT LIKE IT IS

There's a lot more to Cowell than the man we see on screen. Behind the façade of the pantomime villain he is a businessman with a multi-million pound fortune. Nevertheless, he has developed his straight talking persona into an effective on-screen brand that, to some extent, reflects his no-nonsense approach to life outside the studio.

- Find the right industry
- Create a personal brand
- Make honesty the best policy
- Know your limitations

8 MANAGE THE TALENT

Cowell has a good track record in working with artists over longer time frames than the few months following a series of *X Factor* or *Got Talent*. Sitting within the Syco stable are acts such as Westlife and Il Divo who've worked with Cowell over many years – indeed, since well before the arrival of *X Factor* on UK screens. Many of Cowell's wins are short term, but he also looks to long-term talent development.

- Keep the contracts tight
- Know when to be flexible
- Get the best from your assets
- Know when to let go
- Chase where necessary

9   LEARN TO ROLL WITH THE PUNCHES

Cowell's career in the entertainment industry has seen its fair share of setbacks. For the first few years of his career he made little progress and his first taste of success was followed by the bitter pill of a business failure and personal debt. Nevertheless, he not only survived, he has gone on to better things.

- Learn from your parents
- Acknowledge failure
- Resume the climb
- Have your day out of court

10   GET YOUR NAME ON THE TITLE

Cowell has control over his own destiny to a degree that most people in or outside the music and entertainment industries can only dream of. But his autonomy has been hard won. Early attempts at independence came to grief and more recently he has adopted a different strategy. Rather than working independently of the music industry, he has built his businesses in partnership with a corporate, first with BMG and now (following a takeover) with Sony. It has been a rollercoaster ride in terms of ownership.

- Establish the freedom to do what you want
- Become a talent magnet
- Lead with vision
- Own your assets

THE LAST WORD

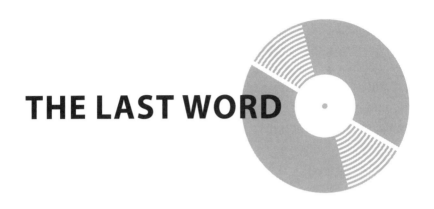

As Cowell sits at his desk, contemplating his newly acquired 50% holding in the reconstituted Syco, he can also look forward confidently to the immediate future.

In the short term, his immediate priority is ensuring that the Syco-owned *X Factor* is a success in the US market. The chances are it will be. With Cowell reprising his UK role on the US judging panel, his popularity in America, coupled with the show's tried and tested formula, should be enough to keep the ratings in the stratosphere.

In the longer term, there's less certainty. All TV formats have a lifespan. In some cases that can be decades but there's always a peak followed by a shallow or precipitous decline.

Falling audiences could pose a particular problem for the Cowell/Syco business model. If fewer people watch *X Factor* then the payback from record sales is likely to be proportionately smaller. Equally important, if the buzz evaporates then there is also a distinct possibility that fewer people will queue up for the auditions. By the law of averages this makes it harder to find top-class acts with long-term career prospects.

For the moment at least, decline seems some way off. Ratings for *X Factor* have remained solid and, in the UK, recent seasons have produced singers with real potential, such as Leona Lewis and Alexandra Burke.

And even if *X Factor* fades, the Cowell model of integrating television and music production is beginning to look like an industry standard. Witness a recent announcement from Tim Bowen, formerly an executive at Sony BMG. His new venture BPM appears to make use of some of the principles of the Syco concept. Primarily aimed at marketing music, its operations will, nonetheless, span film and TV production with the aim of giving acts exposure on complementary media.

This isn't necessarily a new idea. Prior to *Pop Idol*, Cowell's rival and partner Simon Fuller had done a sterling job in selling records by S Club 7 off the back of a TV series featuring the band. Go further back and the producers of the Monkees pulled off the same trick in the 1960s and 1970s.

But with no shows along the lines of *Top of the Pops* on UK peak time television, record companies are having to be ever more creative about getting their acts on air and presenting them in a context that suits their style and audience. Even if the TV talent show format goes off the boil, there are bound to be other formats, and Cowell and his team remain well placed to develop these as the old ones die a natural death.

Meanwhile Syco is not putting all its discs in the TV tie-in rack. A recent signing of 'urban' singer Labarinth was seen by the industry as a sign that the label was ready and willing to take on acts that came from way beyond the world of reality TV. Indeed, announcing the signing, Syco managing director Sonny Takhar acknowledged that the label needed to have a more balanced approach to signing and developing talent.

Cowell will never be popular with music critics. He's always made it clear that his motivation is money rather than music and this has made him a *bête noire* for those who believe that pop music should be a vital and creative force, rather than forgettable entertainment.

But, in an industry that looks back with golden hued nostalgia to the stratospheric record sales of the 1980s and 1990s, Cowell's stock has probably never been higher. True, the chances of seeing a Cowell protégé walking off with a Mercury Prize – the UK's most coveted award for creative artists – are probably akin to a snowball surviving a long, hot day in July. But even if the music he promotes fails to win awards for cutting-edge work, his business approach selling records has been innovative and massively successful.

At least part of that success has been down to his determined and irrepressible visibility as both a TV star and industry executive, while his restless nature has manifested itself in a genuine willingness to innovate. Those characteristics should serve him well in the next decade.

NOTES

THE LIFE AND TIMES OF SIMON COWELL

1   Mostrous, Alexi. 'Simon Cowell's fortune: £123m and counting', *The Times*, 14 November 2009
2   *Ibid.*
3   Newkey-Burden, Chas. *Simon Cowell, The Unauthorized Biography*, Michael O'Mara Books Ltd 2010
4   Johnston, Jenny. 'Revealed: the secrets of Simon Cowell's youth, by his mother', the *Daily Mail*, 29 October 2007
5   'Simon Cowell: I hated school so much I wanted to die', *Now Magazine*, 18 May 2008
6   White, Dominic. 'What you've got to do is win and have hits. You never lose by having hits', the *Daily Telegraph*, 21 December 2006
7   Clark, Nick. 'Music business stages a comeback with first rise in sales for five years', the *Independent*, 27 April 2010

CHAPTER 1

1   Byrne, Ciar. 'Simon Cowell: And the real winner is …', the *Independent*, 16 January 2006
2   Cooper, Anderson. *60 Minutes*, CBS, 18 March 2007
3   Johnston, Jenny. 'Revealed: the secrets of Simon Cowell's youth, by his mother', the *Daily Mail*, 29 October 2007
4   Newkey-Burden, Chas. *Simon Cowell, The Unauthorized Biography*, Michael O'Mara Books Ltd 2010

CHAPTER 2

1   'Cowell extends deal with Sony BMG', *Music Week*, 5 December 2005
2   Cooper, Anderson. *60 Minutes*, CBS, 18 March 2007
3   *New Musical Express* magazine, December 2009
4   *Ibid.*

CHAPTER 3

1   Howe, Jeff. 'Crowdsourcing', *YouTube*, 28 July 2008
2   Khan, Urmee. 'Sharon Osbourne: "I quit *X Factor* because of Danni Minogue"', the *Daily Telegraph*, 16 February 2009
3   Nikkhah, Roya. 'Why Simon Cowell is the real winner of *X Factor*', the *Daily Telegraph*, 14 November 2009

CHAPTER 4

1   Ashton, James. 'Pop impresario Cowell sets out to conquer the world', *The Times*, 24 January 2010
2   Neate, Rupert. 'Talkback Thames boss would like to clone Simon Cowell', the *Daily Telegraph*, 23 January 2010
3   *Ibid.*
4   White, Dominic. 'What you've got to do is win and have hits. You never lose by having hits', the *Daily Telegraph*, 21 December 2006

CHAPTER 5

1   Edgecliffe-Johnson, Anthony. 'Local TV lights up global sets', the *Financial Times*, 12 September 2007
2   Hefferman, Virginia. 'Here Comes the Judge: Take Cover, Would-Be Idols', the *New York Times*, 19 May 2004
3   Wyatt, Edward. 'Cowell Says He Will Leave "Idol"', the *New York Times*, 11 January 2010
4   Newkey-Burden, Chas. *Simon Cowell, The Unauthorized Biography*, Michael O'Mara Books Ltd 2010
5   Edgecliffe-Johnson, Anthony. 'Local TV lights up global sets', the *Financial Times*, 12 September 2007
6   CTV press release 2010
7   Brook, Stephen. 'Britain leads the way in selling global TV formats', the *Guardian*, 5 April 2010

CHAPTER 6

1   Arlidge, John. 'The XX Factor: Simon Cowell teams up with Sir Philip Green', *The Times*, 28 June 2009
2   Garrahan, Matthew. 'Tea With Simon Cowell', the *Financial Times*, 27 July
3   Moules, Jonathan. 'Voice of lucrative experience', the *Financial Times*, 13 June 2007
4   Garrahan, Matthew. 'Cowell and retailer Green join forces', the *Financial Times*, 23 June 2009
5   Sony statement

CHAPTER 7

1   Fulton, Rick. 'Pete Waterman: I don't want Simon Cowell's lifestyle but I'd take over *X Factor* for £1million', the *Daily Record*, 9 September 2009
2   Higgins, Martin. 'Simon Cowell's top 10 cut-downs', *Metro.co.uk*, 12 January 2010
3   Cadwalladr, Carole. 'Susan Boyle: What happened to the dream?', the *Observer*, 30 May 2010
4   *Hollyscoop* website, May 2008
5   Nikkhah, Roya. 'Why Simon Cowell is the real winner of *X Factor*', the *Daily Telegraph*, 14 November 2009
6   Hardy, Rebecca. '"I'm quite odd. I do get very dark moods": Simon Cowell's most revealing – and surprising – interview ever', the *Daily Mail*, 23 May 2009
7   Newkey-Burden, Chas. *Simon Cowell, The Unauthorized Biography*, Michael O'Mara Books Ltd 2010
8   McGinn, Dan. 'Simon Cowell's Managerial Legacy', *Harvard Business School* blog, 27 May 2010
9   Kreiger, Candice. 'Simon Cowell, the new property idol', the *Jewish Chronicle*, 26 November 2009

CHAPTER 8

1   Interview with Simon Cowell, *CNN Larry King Live*, 17 March 2006
2   Bryant, Tom. '*X Factor* exclusive: Secrets of the winner's "£1million contract"', the *Daily Mirror*, 10 December 2008
3   Akbar, Arifa. 'Don't insult Simon Cowell – anywhere in the solar system', the *Independent*, 11 December 2008
4   '*X Factor* contract revealed', the *Belfast Telegraph*, 11 December 2008
5   Simon Cowell talking to Ben Shepherd, *GMTV*, June 2009
6   Leona Lewis artist profile, RCAlabelgroup.co.uk
7   McGarry, Lisa. 'Simon Cowell: "There is a 50/50 chance the *X Factor* winner will flop"', Unrealitytv.co.uk, 14 September 2009
8   Scott, Caroline. 'What happens to *The X Factor* runners up?', *The Times*, 26 April 2009
9   Barber, Richard, 'Rhydian Roberts dumps Simon Cowell – and quits the "Sycobubble"', the *Mail Online*, 9 May 2010

CHAPTER 9

1   Michael Eisner, speech, 19 April 1996
2   Barber, Lynn. 'Simply Simon', the *Observer*, 9 December 2007
3   Byrne, Ciar. 'Simon Cowell: And the real winner is …', the *Independent*, 16 January 2006
4   '*Pop Idol* mogul sues Simon Cowell', *BBC News*, 10 September 2004
5   *Ibid.*
6   *Ibid.*
7   Byrne, Ciar. 'Simon Cowell: And the real winner is …', the *Independent*, 16 January 2006
8   *Ibid.*

CHAPTER 10

1   Newton Dunn, Tom. 'Simon Cowell's vision for a New Britain', the *Sun*, 5 May 2010

2   Barber, Lynn. 'Simply Simon', the *Observer*, 9 December 2007

3   Talbot, Martin. 'Entertainment executive – Cowell talks to *Music Week*', *Music Week*, 2 October 2006

4   'Cowell links with BMG for joint venture label', *Music Week*, 23 September 2000

5   'Idol guru sells S Records in five-year BMG deal', *Music Week*, 10 June 2003

INDEX

Trevor Clawson is a freelance business journalist specializing in fast-growth companies, management, new media, technology and marketing. His work has appeared in the *Guardian*, the *Independent*, *The Sunday Times*, the *Mail on Sunday*, *Director* magazine, *Growing Business* magazine and *Revolution*. Prior to going freelance he edited a business teletext news service

for BBC World television and two magazines – *e.Business* and *PLC Director*. He is also the author of *The Unauthorized Guide to Doing Business the Jamie Oliver Way*.